H_LY SPIRIT

GOD OF ORDER

SCOTT ANIOL

Holy Spirit: God of Order
Copyright © 2024 by Scott Aniol

Published by G3 Press
4979 GA-5
Douglasville, GA 30135
www.G3Min.org

Scripture quotations are from the ESV® Bible (*The Holy Bible, English Standard Version®*), copyright © 2001 by Crossway, a publishing ministry of Good News Publishers. Used by permission. All rights reserved. All emphases in Scripture quotations have been added by the author.

Printed in the United States of America by Graphic Response, Atlanta, GA.

ISBN: 978-1-959908-22-7

Contents

Foreword

"Teach sound doctrine and refute those who contra-dict," the Apostle Paul wrote to his partner and fellow worker in the gospel, Titus (Tit 1:9). Dr. Scott Aniol has done just that in this book on the work of the Holy Spirit of God.

A great swath of professing evangelical Christians to-day believe that "Spirit-led" worship will be unpredictable and experiential. The working of the Holy Spirit will be ev-idenced by heightened emotional states, spontaneous speaking in tongues, new revelation, prophetic dreams, and anything-goes worship services. The less structured and more spontaneous the corporate worship experience, the more certain the Spirit is at work.

Signs and wonders and miracles of healing are also said to be a hallmark of the Spirit-led church. Just as the Holy Spirit empowered Jesus and the Apostles to perform mira-cles of healing, he should be empowering believers to do the same today. The immutability of the Holy Spirit leads, they say, to the inescapable conclusion that the modern church should mirror in every way the churches of the Apostolic era.

Hundreds of millions of professing believers have been taught to expect promptings, hunches, and nudges from the

Holy Spirit. He will even speak to the Christian in a direct, quotable sense. This is a sure sign that the Holy Spirit is at work in the believer's life. In fact, the absence of such activity is deemed a dire warning. Henry Blackaby in his seminal book, *Experiencing God*, writes, "If you have trouble hearing God speak, you are in trouble at the very heart of your Christian experience."[1]

The stakes are high. Hearing from God outside of Scripture is apparently ground-level basics for the Christian. If this is not your norm, you are in trouble.

Dr. Sam Storms is widely regarded to be one of the most careful and cautious theologians within the charismatic camp, yet even he argues that receiving direct communication from the Holy Spirit is a requirement to have intimacy with God. He writes, "To be the recipient of prophetic revelation from God, whether in dreams, impressions, trances, visions, or words of knowledge and words of wisdom can be nothing short of euphoric. The experience brings feelings of nearness to God and a heightened sense of spiritual intimacy that isn't often the case with other of the charismata (spiritual gifts)."[2]

But this is profoundly unbiblical teaching. This divides Christians into classes: the spiritual Haves and Have-Nots. If you receive dreams, visions, and even trances from the

---

[1] Henry T. Blackaby and Claude V. King, *Experiencing God: Knowing and Doing the Will of God* (Nashville: B&H Publishing Group, 2004), 87.

[2] Storms, Sam, *Practicing the Power* (Grand Rapids: Zondervan, 2017), 143.

Holy Spirit, you are a Have. But if you, for example, are a Christian with a Bible, the indwelling of the Holy Spirit, who is gifted in teaching or administration, you are a Have-Not. That's just not very "intimate."

Christians are made to doubt their walk with Christ and even their very salvation if they are not the recipients of these kinds of experiences. Churches are deemed unspiritual and dead if they do not have highly emotionalized services and regularly produce signs, wonders, and miracles of healing.

But these things are not the work of the Holy Spirit. Dr. Aniol persuasively argues from Scripture that the true work of the Holy Spirit is not producing chaos but rather order. The true work of the Holy Spirit does not produce hysterics but rather holiness. The Holy Spirit does not point people to himself but rather to Jesus.

The Holy Spirit is sovereign and is always active. He needs neither our permission nor our activation. The Holy Spirit is no longer bestowing miraculous gifts as he did in the early church, but his work is no less supernatural today than it was then. The Holy Spirit does his divine work through the ordinary and effectual means of grace.

It is the height of irony that the theological camp which claims to have the highest view of the Holy Spirit is also the welcoming home to the most egregious heresies, false prophecies, and chicanery which bring nothing but reproach to his name and confusion to the church.

As cessationists, we are so often told that we do not believe in the power of the Holy Spirit. To the contrary, as cessationists, our view of the Holy Spirit and his work is far too high to lay practices and behavior that is anything but holy at his anthropomorphic feet. As cessationists we cede no ground in our pneumatology to the charismatics.

I invite you to read this book to come into a right understanding of the Person and work of the Holy Spirit. Rightly understanding the orderly and providential work of the Holy Spirit will bring to you immeasurable comfort and benefit as you "grow in the grace and knowledge of our Lord and Savior Jesus Christ" (2 Peter 3:18).

Justin Peters

1

God of Disorder?

"Our church's worship is pretty formal, but I prefer Holy Spirit-led worship."

Such was a comment I overheard once by a young evangelical describing his church's worship service, illustrating a very common perception by many evangelicals today—if the Holy Spirit actively works in worship, the results will be something extraordinary, an experience "quenched" by too much form and order.

But this expectation appears in more than just worship. If you were to ask the average Christian today what our expectation should be regarding how the Holy Spirit works, I believe most Christians would answer something like this: If the Holy Spirit is actively working, his work will be evidenced by some sort of extraordinary experience—intense feelings, inner promptings, miraculous gifts, or even visible manifestations.

As that representative list illustrates, this expectation takes a variety of forms, of course. Let's examine a few of them.

Extraordinary Revelation

A significant way this expectation reveals itself is in common evangelical expectations regarding how God speaks to us and how he reveals his will to us. It is very common in modern evangelicalism, for example, to hear Christians talk about how God "spoke" to them, revealing his will in mystical ways outside his Word.

This teaching characterizes charismatics to be sure, many of which believe that the Holy Spirit still gives revelation with the same level of authority that he did to prophets like Elijah and Isaiah and apostles like John and Paul.[1]

However, more moderate charismatics like Wayne Grudem and Sam Storms argue that while the authoritative canon of Scripture is closed, we ought to still expect "spontaneous revelation from the Holy Spirit" today.[2] In this more moderate view, prophecy today does not have the same sort of inerrancy or authority as biblical prophecy or inspired Scripture, but it is still direct revelation from the Spirit. I am thankful that these men defend the closed canon and the unique authority of Scripture, starkly differentiating their teaching from that of other more dangerous

---

[1] For examples, see John MacArthur, *Strange Fire: The Danger of Offending the Holy Spirit with Counterfeit Worship* (New York: Thomas Nelson, 2013), chap. 6.

[2] Wayne Grudem, *The Gift of Prophecy in the New Testament and Today*, Rev. ed. (Wheaton, IL: Crossway, 2000), 120.

charismatics. Nevertheless, we must still measure their teaching against what the Bible actually teaches.

On the other hand, even many prominent evangelical teachers who claim to believe that prophecy has ceased nevertheless teach that we ought to expect the Holy Spirit to speak directly to us, not with words, and they don't even call it prophecy, but they teach that the Holy Spirit speaks to us through impressions, through promptings, a still small voice, or an inner peace.

Perhaps no single book has done more to spread this kind of expectation among evangelical Christians than Henry Blackaby's *Experiencing God*. Blackaby says, "God has not changed. He still speaks to his people. If you have trouble hearing God speak, you are in trouble at the very heart of your Christian experience."[3] This is someone who claims to believe that prophecy has ceased. Other teachers like Charles Stanley and Priscilla Shirer have taught that we need to learn to listen for God's voice outside of Scripture, we ought to expect to receive "personal divine direction," "detailed guidance," and "intimate leading."[4]

Another way this expectation appears is in common beliefs regarding the doctrine of illumination. Often we hear prayers like, "Lord, please illumine your Word so that we

---

[3] Blackaby and King, *Experiencing God*, 137.

[4] Priscilla Shirer, *Discerning the Voice of God: How to Recognize When He Speaks* (Chicago: Moody Publishers, 2012), 18, 20.

can understand what it says," or other similar language. Intentional or not, many believers seem to expect that the Spirit is going to help us understand what Scripture means or that he is going to "speak" to us specific ways that the Word applies to our personal situations. However, as we will see in this book, neither of these are what the biblical doctrine of illumination means.

The fact is that many Christians today think that supernatural experiences were just the normal, expected way God spoke to everyone in biblical times. Here's Henry Blackaby again:

> The testimony of the Bible from Genesis to Revelation is that God speaks to his people, . . . and you can anticipate that he will be speaking to you also.[5]

Charles Stanley argued,

> [God] loves us just as much as he loved the people of Old and New Testament days. . . . We need his definite and deliberate direction for our lives, as did Joshua, Moses, Jacob, or Noah. As his children, we need his counsel for effective decision making. Since he wants us to make

---

[5] Blackaby and King, *Experiencing God*, 57.

the right choices, he is still responsible for providing accurate data, and that comes through his speaking to us.[6]

These are not charismatics or continuationists. These are teachers who claim to be cessationists, and yet they insist that we ought to expect to hear from God outside his Word. And yet, this really is no different from how moderate continuationists define prophecy today.

In fact, Tom Schreiner admits as much in his book, *Spiritual Gifts*. Schreiner says this:

> What most call prophecy in churches today, in my judgment, isn't the New Testament gift of prophecy. . . . It is better to characterize what is happening today as the sharing of impressions rather than prophecy. God may impress something on a person's heart and mind, and he may use such impressions to help others in their spiritual walk. It is a matter of definition; *what some people call prophecies are actually impressions, where someone senses that God is leading them to speak to someone or to make some kind of statement about a situation.*[7]

And Schreiner even admits that this is not much different from the moderate continuationist theology of prophecy:

---

[6] Charles F. Stanley, *How to Listen to God* (Grand Rapids: Thomas Nelson, 2002), 3.

[7] Thomas R. Schreiner, *Spiritual Gifts: What They Are and Why They Matter* (Nashville: B&H Publishing Group, 2018), 118. Emphasis added.

The difference between cessationists and continuationists is in some ways insignificant at the practical level when it comes to prophecy, *for what continuationists call prophecy, cessationists call impressions.* As a cessationist, I affirm that God may speak to his people through impressions. And there are occasions where impressions are startlingly accurate.[8]

I respect Tom Schreiner greatly, but the problem is that teachings about Holy Spirit impressions such as these are not based on any Scripture at all. Rather, they use phrases like, "We have all experienced this kind of thing," "these impressions are startingly accurate, so they must be from God," or they quote a few vague statements by Spurgeon, Edwards, or Lloyd Jones that sound like they believed in such impressions.

I would estimate that a vast majority of evangelical Christians today believe that the Holy Spirit speaks through promptings and impressions, especially with regard to his will for our lives. If you want to truly know God's will, then the Bible is not enough. The Bible does not tell you specifics about God's "secret will" for your life, so if you want to know it, you need to learn to listen to God's voice. Not audible words of course, not prophecy—we're cessationists after all, but we ought to expect to receive nudges

---

[8] Schreiner, *Spiritual Gifts*, 119. Emphasis added.

or impressions from the Spirit, an inner peace that will give us guidance.

Extraordinary Gifts

In addition to receiving new revelation from the Holy Spirit, many professing Christians today also believe that the Holy Spirit continues to gift believers with special abilities like healing and speaking in tongues.

The first appearance of tongues in Scripture, Acts 2, is the single most important text for discerning the nature of this gift. Notice, first, that Luke states in verse 4 that the apostles and 120 followers "began to speak in other tongues as the Spirit gave them utterance." The word "tongues" there is the Greek term *glossais*, which is the word used to describe the literal tongue organ in the mouth, so at this point the text is not clear as to what exactly "tongues" means.

But in verse 8, the Jews say, "And how is it that we hear, each of us in his own native language?" Here the word "language" is the term *dialecto*, from which we get our English word "dialect," and it is clear that they are referring to distinct, known languages—different "dialects" from the various nations from which they came, listed in verses 10-11.

What's more, these same Jews say at the end of verse 11, "we hear them telling in our own tongues the mighty works of God." The word "tongues" here is the same as verse 4—

glossais, yet it is clear that they are using it interchangeably with *dialecto*—"languages" in verse 8. In other words, what is apparent in this first appearance of tongues in Scripture is that "tongues" and "languages" are exactly the same thing. They are interchangeable. Therefore, the gift of tongues is the ability to speak in known languages that the speaker himself does not know.

This biblical definition of tongues as speaking known languages is a far cry from the practice of tongues by charismatics today. In fact, even Charles Parham, the preacher connected with the first supposed case of tongues that sparked the modern Pentecostal movement, claimed that Agnes Ozman spoke in Chinese, though this was quickly proven false.[9] Even D. A. Carson, a continuationist, acknowledges that "Modern tongues are lexically uncommunicative and the few instances of reported modern [speaking in foreign languages] are so poorly attested that no weight can be laid on them."[10]

But as with the matter of extraordinary revelation, moderate continuationists also defend the continuation of the gift of tongues. And like with revelation, they often do so on the basis that there are two different kinds of tongues.

---

[9] Vinson Synan, *The Century of the Holy Spirit: 100 Years of Pentecostal and Charismatic Renewal, 1901–2001* (Nashville: Thomas Nelson, 2001), 88.

[10] D. A. Carson, *Showing the Spirit: A Theological Exposition of 1 Corinthians 12-14* (Grand Rapids: Baker Book House, 1987), 84.

They agree that tongues in Acts 2 were known languages, but they insist that tongues in 1 Corinthians 14 were something different. For example, Sam Storms argues,

> Acts 2 is the only text in the New Testament where tongues-speech consists of foreign languages not previously known by the speaker. This is an important text, yet there is no reason to think Acts 2, rather than, say, 1 Corinthians 14, is the standard by which all occurrences of tongues-speech must be judged.[11]

According to Storms and other continuationists, the Spirit continues to give the gift of tongues today as a means of personal private devotion to God. In fact, Storms says that Christians have "a moral and biblical obligation" to seek spiritual gifts like this.[12]

Modern charismatics also claim the Spirit still gives the gift of healing. As with revelation and tongues, it is important to define what healing is biblically. When examining cases of healing in Scripture, it is clear that healings in Scripture were instantaneous. Once a person was declared healed, he did not have to wait for a period of time before he was completely healed. This healing was no gradual process. Furthermore, healings are always of diseases that are

---

[11] Sam Storms, *The Beginner's Guide to Spiritual Gifts*, 2nd ed. (Minneapolis, MN: Bethany House Publishers, 2013), 180.

[12] Storms, *The Beginner's Guide to Spiritual Gifts*, 157.

untreatable like blindness or lameness or even death. Healings were also complete, and they reversed all of the damage caused by whatever malady the individual suffered.

What is also evident from biblical healings is that those who heal do not do it of their own power or even of their own initiative. In fact, they have no control over the timing of when healings would be performed. For instance, even though the apostle Paul performed many spectacular miracles of healing, he endured a thorn in the flesh until the end of his life (2 Cor 12:7-9). He also apparently could not heal Epaphroditus, though he prayed for him (Phil 2:25-30). In other words, no individual permanently had "the gift of healing," but the Spirit did gift individuals with the ability to heal in certain circumstances according to his divine will.

Of course, on the one hand are the faith healers like Aimee Semple McPherson, Oral Roberts, and Benny Hinn, who have held extravagant healing meetings, complete with "slaying people in the spirit" and other frenzied chaos. The "healings" reported from such meetings are highly suspect.[13]

But like with revelation and tongues, more moderate orthodox charismatics also teach that Spirit-given healing continues today. For example, Sam Storms teaches that the Spirit gifts certain individuals in certain circumstances a

---

[13] See MacArthur, *Strange Fire*, chap. 8.

special measure of faith by which their prayers can produce supernatural healing.[14]

I raise examples of more moderate charismatics like Wayne Grudem and Sam Storms, not to lump them together with the prosperity gospel heretics—far from it. These men are orthodox evangelical teachers whose writing in many areas I find helpful. Rather, I raise them to illustrate what I believe to be confusion even among otherwise orthodox individuals regarding how we ought to expect the Holy Spirit to work today.

Extraordinary Worship

Likely the most prevalent form of this expectation revolves around my opening illustration: worship. Arguably, the default expectation of contemporary evangelical worshipers is that the Holy Spirit works in worship in such a way so as to create an extraordinary experience, well expressed in the popular worship song by Bryan and Katie Torwalt:

Holy Spirit, You are welcome here
Come flood this place and fill the atmosphere
Your glory, God, is what our hearts long for

---

[14] Storms, *The Beginner's Guide to Spiritual Gifts*, 70.

To be overcome by Your presence, Lord[15]

As D. A. Carson notes, "At least some Corinthians wanted to measure their maturity by the intensity of their spiritual experiences."[16]

Many theologians and authors who have helped to shape contemporary evangelical worship embody a theology of the Holy Spirit's primary work as that of making God's presence known. For example, Wayne Grudem argues, "The work of the Holy Spirit is to manifest the active presence of God in the world, and especially the church. . . . It seems that one of his primary purposes in the new covenant age," Grudem continues, "is to manifest the presence of God, to give indications that make the presence of God known. . . . To be in the Holy Spirit is really to be in an atmosphere of God's manifested presence."[17] Zac Hicks agrees: "The Holy Spirit has an agenda in manifesting his presence to us."[18] Bob Kauflin believes that "there are times, of course, when we become unexpectedly aware of the Lord's presence in an intense way. A sudden wave of peace

---

[15] "Holy Spirit," 2011, https://songselect.ccli.com/Songs/6087919/holy-spirit. This is a CCLI Top 10 song.

[16] Carson, *Showing the Spirit*, 108.

[17] Wayne Grudem, *Systematic Theology* (Grand Rapids: Zondervan, 1995), 634, 641, 648.

[18] Zac M. Hicks, *The Worship Pastor: A Call to Ministry for Worship Leaders and Teams* (Grand Rapids: Zondervan, 2016), 33.

comes over us. An irrepressible joy rises up from the depths of our soul."[19] "None of us," Kauflin insists, "should be satisfied with our present experience of the Spirit's presence and power."[20]

This expectation is certainly not new; theologians such as John Owen and Jonathan Edwards addressed the religious "enthusiasts" of their day.[21] However, the contemporary iteration is rooted in a Pentecostal theology of the Holy Spirit's work. In their insightful *Concise History of Contemporary Worship, Lovin' on Jesus*, Swee Hong Lim and Lester Ruth convincingly demonstrate that Pentecostalism, with its "revisioning of a New Testament emphasis upon the active presence and ministry of the Holy Spirit," is one of five key sources of contemporary worship.[22] They suggest that "Pentecostalism's shaping of contemporary worship has been both through its own internal development and through an influencing of other Protestants in worship

---

[19] Bob Kauflin, *True Worshipers: Seeking What Matters to God* (Wheaton, IL: Crossway Books, 2015), 133.

[20] Bob Kauflin, *Worship Matters: Leading Others to Encounter the Greatness of God* (Wheaton: Crossway Books, 2008), 84–85.

[21] See Ryan J. Martin, "'Violent Motions of Carnal Affections': Jonathan Edwards, John Owen, and Distinguishing the Work of the Spirit from Enthusiasm," *Detroit Baptist Seminary Journal* 15 (2010): 99–116.

[22] Swee Hong Lim and Lester Ruth, *Lovin' on Jesus: A Concise History of Contemporary Worship* (Nashville: Abingdon Press, 2017), 17–18. The other four are youth ministry, baby boomers, Jesus People, and church growth missiology.

piety and practice," including the following ways its theology has shaped contemporary worship:

1. mainstreaming the desire to be physical and expressive in worship
2. highlighting intensity as a liturgical virtue
3. a certain expectation of experience to the forms of contemporary worship, and
4. a musical sacramentality [that] raises the importance of the worship set as well as the musicians leading this set.[23]

They explain, "Pentecostalism contributed contemporary worship's sacramentality, that is, both the expectation that God's presence could be encountered in worship and the normal means by which this encounter would happen," creating an "expectation for encountering God, active and present through the Holy Spirit."[24] Daniel Albrecht agrees: "The presence of the Holy Spirit then is fundamental to a Pentecostal perspective of worship. The conviction that the Spirit is present in worship is one of the deepest beliefs in a Pentecostal liturgical vision. The expectancy of the Spirit's presence is often palpable in the liturgy. . . . Their liturgical rites and sensibilities encourage becoming consciously

[23] Lim and Ruth, *Lovin' on Jesus*, 18.
[24] Lim and Ruth, *Lovin' on Jesus*, 18.

present to God—even as God's presence is expected to become very real in worship."[25]

Monique M. Ingalls agrees with this assessment after her ten year study (2007 to 2017) of contemporary worship in several different settings.[26] She notes the connection between centrality of contemporary worship music and the desire of worshipers to experience "a personal encounter with God during congregational singing."[27] Indeed, an expected experience of the Holy Spirit's active presence is often directly tied to music, specifically to the "flow" of the emotional expressiveness of the worship music. Hicks suggests, "Part of leading a worship service's flow . . . involves keeping the awareness of God's real, abiding presence before his worshipers. As all of the elements of worship pass by, the one constant—the True Flow—is the presence of the Holy Spirit himself." This kind of flow, according to Hicks, "lies in understanding and guiding your worship service's emotional journey."[28] "Grouping songs in such a way that

---

[25] Daniel E. Albrecht, "Worshiping and the Spirit: Transmuting Liturgy Pentecostally," in *The Spirit in Worship—Worship in the Spirit*, ed. Teresa Berger and Bryan D. Spinks (Collegeville, MN: Liturgical Press, 2009), 239.

[26] Monique M. Ingalls, *Singing the Congregation: How Contemporary Worship Music Forms Evangelical Community* (New York: Oxford University Press, 2018).

[27] Ingalls, *Singing the Congregation*, 85.

[28] Hicks, *The Worship Pastor*, 184.

they flow together," worship leader Carl Tuttle explains, "is essential to a good worship experience."[29] The goal and expectation of any worship service, according to Barry Griffing, "is to bring the congregational worshipers into a corporate awareness of God's manifest presence."[30] James Steven notes, "By investing heavily in particular signs of the Spirit's presence, such as ecstatic physical patterns of behavior, church members define the Spirit by the empirical measurement of particular phenomena, which if absent imply that the Spirit has not 'turned up.'"[31] For Pentecostals and other continuationists, this expectation includes miraculous gifts such as tongues and prophecy, but even for other evangelicals who do not hold to a continuationist position on miraculous gifts, the default expectation is that the Holy Spirit will manifest God's presence in other extraordinary ways such as a heightened experience of emotional euphoria.

---

[29] Carl Tuttle, "Song Selection & New Song Introduction," in *Worship Leaders Training Manual* (Anaheim, CA: Worship Resource Center/Vineyard Ministries International, 1987), 141.

[30] Barry Griffing, "Releasing Charismatic Worship," in *Restoring Praise & Worship to the Church* (Shippensburg, PA: Revival Press, 1989), 92.

[31] James Steven, "The Spirit in Contemporary Charismatic Worship," in *The Spirit in Worship—Worship in the Spirit*, ed. Teresa Berger and Bryan D. Spinks (Collegeville, MN: Liturgical Press, 2009), 258.

Thus, worship in which the Holy Spirit is directly active is often necessarily connected with spontaneity and "freedom" of form. Worship that is structured and regulated is the opposite of "Spirit-led" worship in this view. As Lim and Ruth note, most contemporary worship, impacted as it is by this understanding of the Holy Spirit's work in worship, considers "extemporaneity as a mark of worship that is true and of the Holy Spirit, that is, worship in Spirit and truth (Jn 4:24). This view of extemporaneity" they note, "has been held widely within Free Church ways of worship."[32] What Albrecht observes of Pentecostal worship has become the standard expectation for most of evangelicalism:

> In the midst of radical receptivity, an encounter with the Holy Spirit may occur. Pentecostals envision such encounters as integral to the worship experience. While an overwhelming or overpowering experience of/in the Spirit is neither rare nor routine for a particular Pentecostal worshiper, the experiential dimension of worship is fundamental. The liturgical vision sees God as present in the service; consequently,

---

[32] Lim and Ruth, *Lovin' on Jesus*, 38.

Pentecostals reason that a direct experience of God is a normal expectation.[33]

Contemporary evangelicalism, I believe, has been thoroughly Pentecostalized with the expectation that if the Holy Spirit is active and working, then we will witness extraordinary effects ranging from direct revelation, special gifting, and emotional euphoria.

The question is whether this is what the Bible teaches we ought to expect today.

---

[33] Albrecht, "Worshiping and the Spirit: Transmuting Liturgy Pentecostally," 240.

2

God of Order

Ultimately, I am convinced that a charismatic theology of the Holy Spirit has infected most of evangelicalism in ways we don't often recognize. And I am also convinced that one of the primary reasons for this is actually a neglect in clear teaching about who the Holy Spirit is and what we should expect his normal work to be according to the Word of God. Carl F. H. Henry was right when he observed, "The modern openness to charismatic emphasis is directly traceable to the neglect by mainstream Christian denominations of an adequate doctrine of the Holy Spirit."[1] Sinclair Ferguson noted concerning views regarding the Holy Spirit in 1996, "It is a remarkable fact of recent church history that convictions which were controversial in my student days in the 1960s and 70s have now become so broadly adopted that it is the mainstream views of those days which are now regarded as controversial."[2]

---

[1] Carl F. H. Henry, *God, Revelation and Authority: Volume 4: God Who Speaks and Shows* (Wheaton, IL: Crossway, 1999), 284.

[2] Sinclair B. Ferguson, *The Holy Spirit* (Downers Grove, IL: IVP Academic, 1997), 13.

The remedy to this problem, then, is to clearly articulate what the Bible tells us will be the Holy Spirit's normal work, and that is what I intend to do in this book. This book is not a book on the doctrine of the Holy Spirit generally, but rather a focused consideration of the Holy Spirit's *work* in history.[3] But allow me here to first briefly affirm core assertions concerning the nature of the Holy Spirit's *person* as a foundation for this study on his work.

Who Is the Holy Spirit?

God exists eternally in three persons: Father, Son, and Holy Spirit. These three persons exist simultaneously in one divine being, having the same attributes and worthy of the same worship and honor. God does not have three parts, three natures, or three wills; God has one nature and one will. Yet the one God exists in three divine persons. The Father eternally begets the Son (Ps 2:7, Jn 5:26); the Son is eternally begotten of the Father (Jn 1:14, 3:16); and the Holy Spirit eternally proceeds from the Father and the Son (Jn 14:26, 15:26). One God existing in three divine persons.

Thus, the Holy Spirit is coequal and coeternal with the Father and Son. He is called God (Acts 5:1-4), he is named in the trinitarian titles as equal with the Father and the Son

---

[3] For a thorough study of the doctrine of the Holy Spirit, I highly recommend Ferguson, *The Holy Spirit*.

(Mt 28:19, 2 Cor 3:18, 1 Pt 1:2), and he possesses the attributes of God such as eternality (Heb 9:14), omnipresence (Ps 139:7–10), omnipotence (Gn 1:2, Lk 1:35), omniscience (1 Cor 2:10–11), holiness (Eph 4:30), and truth (1 Jn 5:6).

The Holy Spirit is a personal being. He possesses the essential characteristics of personality such as life (Rom 8:2), intelligence (1 Cor 2:10–11), freedom (1 Cor 12:11), purpose (1 Cor 12:11), action (Jn 16:8), self-consciousness (Acts 13:2), and affections (Eph 4:30).

Since our focus in this book is on the *works* of the Holy Spirit, it is also important here that we affirm biblical teaching regarding the relationship between the one nature of God and the activities of the three divine persons. As we discuss the works of the Holy Spirit, we cannot imagine that the Spirit is a person acting with a will that is distinct from the other persons of the godhead. In other words, it is not as if the Holy Spirit acts independently of the Father and the Son. Rather, since God has only one nature, he has only one will. Everything that God does, the Spirit does, and everything that the Spirit does, God does.

Jesus himself states this clearly of himself when he says, "whatever the Father does, that the Son does likewise" (Jn 5:19). Basil of Caesarea summarized this important doctrine specifically regarding the Holy Spirit:

> In all things, the Holy Spirit is inseparable and wholly incapable of being parted from the Father and the Son.

. . . In every operation the Spirit is closely conjoined with, and inseparable from, the Father and the Son.[4]

So how, then, can we refer to "works of the Holy Spirit"? In referring to the Holy Spirit's works, we are not referring to activities that are independent of the other divine persons. Rather, we are referring to particular aspects of one divine action that Scripture *appropriates* to the Holy Spirit. The one undivided God always acts according to his one undivided will, but often Scripture focuses attention on a particular aspect of the undivided action appropriated by one of the divine persons.

In other words, every undivided action of God is performed by each divine person in accordance with his eternal relation to the other persons. I noted above that the Son is eternally begotten of the Father, and the Spirit eternally proceeds from the Father and the Son. On the basis of these eternal relations, Herman Bavinck notes,

All the works of God . . . have one single Author, namely, God. But they come into being through the cooperation of the three persons, each of whom plays a specific role and fulfills a special task, both in the works of creation and in those of redemption and sanctification. All

---

[4] Basil of Caesarea, *The Book of Saint Basil on the Spirit*, NPNF 2, n.d., 8:23.

things proceed from the Father, are accomplished by the Son, and are completed in the Holy Spirit."[5]

In fact, that very way of understanding the Holy Spirit's "special task" as that of *completing* the works of God is going to help us discern the nature of what the Holy Spirit has done and continues to do in history.

The Bible certainly teaches that the Holy Spirit is God who is worthy of all glory and worship, and as God, the Holy Spirit may certainly work in whatever ways he deems fit. However, if we believe that Holy Scripture is inspired, inerrant, authoritative, and sufficient, then we must also believe that biblical revelation will tell us how the Holy Spirit has chosen to work in human history. All of our expectations regarding how the Holy Spirit will normally work today must be measured against the teachings of Holy Scripture.

Actions of the Holy Spirit in Scripture

Ultimately, current expectations concerning the Holy Spirit's work in worship must derive, not from experience, but from Scripture. Too often in modern evangelicalism, expectations regarding how the Holy Spirit works are based upon anecdotes, stories, or other testimonies of

[5] Herman Bavinck, *Reformed Dogmatics*, vol. 2 (Grand Rapids: Baker Books, 2004), 319.

people's experiences rather on what the Bible actually teaches. As illustrated in the last chapter, this is just as true of those who claim to be cessationists as it is of charismatics.

In his book, *The Work of the Holy Spirit*, Abraham Kuyper presents several helpful reasons we must not develop our theology of the Holy Spirit on the basis of experience.[6] First, it is difficult to discern the difference between people whose experience we believe to be "pure and healthy" and those we "put aside as strained and unhealthful." We may think we have reasons for trusting one person's experience over another, but at the end of the day our determination of which experiences to believe is subjective. We need a more objective standard than anyone's personal experience, no matter how much we trust them.

Second, "the testimony of believers presents only the dim outlines of the work of the Holy Spirit." Even if a person is accurately describing their experience, what they describe is only their finite perception of the effects of his work and can never capture the fullness of what he does.

Third, great men in church history who have spoken "clearly, truthfully, and forcibly" about the Spirit's work in their lives, in contrast to those who speak "confusingly," do so by using language taken directly from Scripture. In other

---

[6] Abraham Kuyper, *The Work of the Holy Spirit* (New York: Funk & Wagnalls, 1900), 4ff.

words, as we will discuss, many of the Spirit's works are indeed experiential, but even in describing our subjective experiences of the Spirit's work, it is best to use objective language from Scripture.

Finally, when people do describe their experiences in words other than Scripture, this is typically because of the influence of some strong preacher or teacher whose language these people begin to borrow. In other words, the language we use to describe the Spirit's experiential work will come from somewhere; it is best that our language come from Scripture itself rather than from someone else.

For all of these reasons, we cannot derive our expectations regarding how the Holy Spirit works from our own experiences or other people's testimonies of their personal experiences. Rather, we must align our expectations of the Holy Spirit's work with the teachings of Holy Scripture. In order to lay such a biblical foundation, I'll survey here how the Bible broadly characterizes the activities of God especially appropriated to the Holy Spirit that we'll be working through in this book.

Scripture contains roughly 250 explicit descriptions of the Holy Spirit's actions, 90 in the Old Testament, and 165 in the New Testament.[7] Overwhelmingly, the dominant

---

[7] Thanks to PhD students in a seminar I taught on the Holy Spirit and Worship at Southwestern Baptist Theological Seminary, and especially my graduate assistant John Gray, for helping to compile and organize this biblical data. The list contains only direct actions ascribed to

action ascribed to the Holy Spirit in both Testaments is the giving of revelation (37 times in the OT and 64 times in the NT). God the Spirit speaks through prophets and apostles, and ultimately inspires the Holy Scriptures themselves (2 Tm 3:16, 2 Pt 1:21).

In the Old Testament, much of the revelation of God given to his people through human prophets occurs after the Holy Spirit "came upon" them. For example, this is true of Joseph (Gn 41:38), the elders of Israel (Nm 11:25), Balaam (Nm 24:2), and Saul (1 Sm 10:10). David, too, declared, "The Spirit of the Lord speaks by me; his word is on my tongue" (2 Sm 23:2), and several places in the New Testament attribute David's prophecies directly to the Holy Spirit (Mt 22:43; Mk 12:36; Acts 1:16, 4:8). And certainly other cases of divine revelation, though not explicitly attributed to the Holy Spirit, were his work. For example, Nehemiah 9:20 describes all of the prophecy given to the Israelites in the wilderness as instruction from God's good Spirit.

In the New Testament, prophetic words are almost always described as a work of the Holy Spirit, including those given to Elizabeth (Lk 1:41), Zechariah (Lk 1:67), Simeon (Lk 2:25-26), Stephen (Acts 6:10), and even Jesus himself (Acts 1:2).

---

the Holy Spirit, not necessarily assumed effects of his actions. I examined each case and categorized the actions based on similarity.

Likewise, he guides the apostles into the truth (Jn 14:26, 16:13) necessary to establish Christian doctrine and set the church in order (1 Tm 3:15). Jesus had promised them that the Spirit would speak through them (Mt 10:20, Mk 13:11, Lk 12:12), and so several apostles are specifically identified as those through whom the Spirit gave revelation, including Peter (Acts 10:19) and Paul (Acts 20:23).

Second in order of frequency in the OT and third in the NT is special empowerment given to individual leaders whom God has called to perform special ministry on his behalf, often closely associated with giving revelation. This act of the Holy Spirit occurs 20 times in the OT and 18 times in the NT, describing the Spirit's work upon men like Moses (Nm 11:17), Joshua (Dt 34:9), judges (Jgs 6:34, 13:25), and prophets (1 Kgs 18:12). Likewise, in the New Testament, the Spirit uniquely empowered Jesus Christ (Jn 1:32), John the Baptist (Lk 1:15), and the apostles (Acts 2:4).

Actions of the Holy Spirit in the OT fall off considerably in frequency after the top two categories. They can be described as follows: The Holy Spirit participated in creation (Gn 1:2, Jb 33:4, Ps 104:30), gifted Bezalel and Oholiab with skill to build the tabernacle (Ex 31:1–5, 35:30–35), and dwelt in the midst of Israel (Neh 9:20, Hag 2:5; cf. Ex 29:45).

In the NT, however, the second most frequent action of the Holy Spirit after revelation is the sanctification of believers, appearing at least 24 times. This work of the Spirit characterizes Spirit-filling (Acts 6:3, 11:24, Eph 5:18) and describes the Spirit's work to progressively produce holy fruit in a believer's life (Rom 15:16, Gal 5:22). In the NT the Holy Spirit also indwells (17 times), regenerates (13 times), assures (5 times), convicts (2 times), and illuminates (2 times).

Finally, Romans 12 and 1 Corinthians 12–14 discuss gifts that are given to believers; 1 Corinthians 12 explains that these gifts are given "through the Spirit" (v. 8) or "by the one Spirit" (v. 9), and chapter 14 calls them "manifestations of the Spirit" (v. 12). Since these passages explicitly ascribe the giving of these gifts to the Holy Spirit, other passages that discuss such gifts may also safely be attributed to a work of the Holy Spirit (e.g., 1 Tm 4:14, 2 Tm 1:6).

Ordinary but Divine

As we begin to characterize the nature of the Spirit's work among us, it is important to define some terms we will use. On the one hand, I will use the contrasting terms *extraordinary* and *ordinary*. By *extraordinary*, I mean works of the Spirit that are unique to certain time periods or individuals. They are out of the ordinary—unusual, unexpected, and surprising. In contrast, *ordinary* works are those the Spirit has performed in the past and continues to perform in the present. These works occur with regularity and ought to be our expectation of how the Holy Spirit will normally work.

However, it is important to note that even *ordinary* works of the Spirit are nevertheless still *divine*. To call them *ordinary* is in no way to imply that they are any less *wondrous*. Every work accomplished by the Spirit is divine, which is to say that these works could be accomplished *only* by God himself. I am going to be arguing that the Spirit normally works in *ordinary* ways today, but please do not hear me implying that we ought not marvel at the ways the Spirit does continue to work today. Indeed, the divine works accomplished by the Spirit would not take place accept through him, and for this reason alone we ought to marvel at everything he does.

I will also use the contrasting terms *supernatural* and *natural*. By *supernatural*, I mean works of the Spirit which involve what Rolland McCune describes as "a suspension, a bypassing, or even an outright contravention of the natural order."[8] Supernatural acts are works like stopping the sun, parting the sea, immediately healing physical ailments, speaking directly to men, or causing men to speak in languages they have never learned. By *natural*, I mean works of the Spirit that "operate within the natural realm of order even though God's hand of providence is involved."[9] But again, it is important for us to recognize that even when the

---

[8] Rolland D. McCune, "A Biblical Study of Tongues and Miracles," *Central Bible Quarterly* 19 (1976): 15.

[9] James F Stitzinger, "Spiritual Gifts: Definitions and Kinds," *TMSJ* 14, no. 2 (Fall 2003): 161.

Holy Spirit works providentially through natural means, his work is no less divine or wondrous. The fact that the sun rose this morning is natural, but it is nevertheless a divine act.

Finally, it is also important to distinguish between works that are *judicial, experiential,* or *external. Judicial* works of the Spirit are objective realities that the Spirit accomplishes, but they are not works of which we would be experientially aware. *Experiential* works of the Spirit are those that impact our daily experience, and thus we are aware of their effects. *External* works are those with visible effects that are observable even to other people. And once again, works of the Spirit in all three categories are equally divine and praiseworthy.

The importance as we examine works of the Spirit in Scripture is that everything the Spirit does is a divine work that should cause us to marvel, though some of his works are ordinary activities he accomplishes through natural means, and not all have external effects.

Characterizing the Holy Spirit's Work

Taking all of the biblical data concerning the Holy Spirit's work throughout history into account, there is no doubt that he sometimes works in extraordinary, supernatural, observable ways. Yet as we will see, extraordinary works of the Spirit are not the ordinary way God works his sovereign will through the course of biblical history. When extraordinary experiences occur, they happen during significant transitional stages in the outworking of God's plan. They have specific purposes, and once those purposes are fulfilled, they cease.

Rather, the ordinary work of the Holy Spirit throughout Scripture is better characterized, not as *extraordinary experience* but rather as an *ordering* of the plan and people of God. Indeed, as I will demonstrate in this book, this overarching characteristic of *ordering* describes much, if not all, of what the Holy Spirit does throughout Scripture, including giving revelation, creating life (both physical and spiritual), and sanctifying individual believers. Louis Berkhof helpfully summarizes the Holy Spirit's work in this way, with particular attention to the other divine persons:

> In general it may be said that it is the special task of the Holy Spirit *to bring things to completion by acting immediately upon and in the creature.* Just as he himself is the person who completes the Trinity, so his work is the completion of God's contact with his creatures and the consummation of the work of God in every sphere. It follows the work of the Son, just as the work of the Son follows that of the Father.[10]

---

[10] Louis Berkhof, *Systematic Theology* (Grand Rapids: Eerdmans, 1938), 98. Emphasis added.

My goal in the rest of the book is to progress through each major category of the Holy Spirit's activities in Scripture, assessing their role, and helping us to discern that *we should expect the Spirit to normally work today in ways that bring order and completion to the plan and people of God.*

3

Creation

The first instance of the Spirit's work appears in the opening verses of Scripture.

> In the beginning, God created the heavens and the earth. [2] The earth was without form and void, and darkness was over the face of the deep. And the Spirit of God was hovering over the face of the waters. (Gn 1:1-2)

On day one of creation, God created all matter, time, and space. Think about it—before the first day of creation, all that existed was the triune God. There was not matter, time, or space. God created all of that on the first day.

But as Genesis 1:2 tells us, that space and matter—heaven and earth—was "without form and void." Simply creating matter and space did not mean they were yet arranged in such a way so as to be inhabitable by human beings.

And so, it was the Spirit of God who hovered over the face of the waters as the person of the triune God who brought order to creation. The Hebrew term *rûach* can mean "breath," "wind," or "spirit," depending on the context. The same is true in the New Testament of the term *pneuma*. We can have confidence that the term in Genesis 1:2 refers to the Holy Spirit because of the verb "hovering," which would not fit "wind" or "breath." Moses uses the same verb to describe God "hovering" over his people at the end of the Pentateuch as well, which appears to be a deliberate parallel with the opening verses of the Pentateuch (Dt 32:11). Additionally, as we will soon note, Moses portrays deliberate parallels between the Spirit's work in creating the world and his work in the creation of the tabernacle, further evidence that he intended *rûach* to refer to the Holy Spirit in Genesis 1:2. Similarly, Job states, "By his wind [*rûach*] the heavens were made fair" (26:13), and Job 33:4 clearly refers to the divine Spirit when it states, "The Spirit [*rûach*] of God has made me, and the breath of the Almighty gives me life."

In other words, in the opening words of Scripture we find the Spirit of God actively involved in the work of creation. Indeed, in the opening chapter of Genesis we find all three persons of the triune God active in creation: God [the Father] created the heavens and the earth, he did so through his Word [the Son], and the work was brought to completion by his Spirit. As we saw in the last chapter, these appropriations of the work of creation to persons of the godhead reflect their eternal relations of origin. Psalms 33:6 portrays this trinitarian act of creation: "By the *word* of the Lord the heavens were made, and by the *breath* [*rûach*] of his mouth all their host." So all three persons of the god-head were involved in creation, and as is true with all of God's works, God performed the work through the Son, and that work was brought to perfection by the Spirit. As John Owen observes, "Whereas the order of operation among the distinct persons depends on the order of their subsistence in the blessed Trinity, in every great work of God, the concluding, completing, perfecting acts are ascribed unto the Holy Ghost."[1]

Thus, in the six days of creation, the Holy Spirit of God brought order to the cosmos—he brought to completion and perfection the creative activity of God. J. I. Packer describes the work of the Spirit here as molding "creation into shape."[2] Boyd Hunt describes the Spirit's work as creating "order and beauty."[3] The Spirit fit the materials of the universe together in such a way that they exhibited the beauty and orderliness of God, which describes all of what the Spirit characteristically does. As Ferguson notes, "the Spirit orders (or re-orders) and ultimately beautifies God's creation."[4] Graham Cole summarizes, "Creation and its

---

[1] John Owen, *The Works of John Owen*, ed. William H. Goold, vol. 3 (Edinburgh: T&T Clark, 1862), 94.

[2] J. I. Packer, *Keep in Step with the Spirit: Finding Fullness in Our Walk with God*, Rev ed (Grand Rapids: Baker Books, 2005), 51.

[3] Boyd Hunt, *Redeemed!: Eschatological Redemption and the Kingdom of God* (Nashville: Baptist Sunday School Board, 1993), 32.

[4] Ferguson, *The Holy Spirit*, 22.

sustenance are the work of the Spirit as the Spirit implements the divine purposes in nature and history."[5]

This orderliness is reflected in the Greek term *cosmos*, which the Greek translation of the Old Testament uses to characterize the finished work of creation: "Thus the heavens and the earth were finished, and all the host [*cosmos*] of them" (Gn 2:1). Paul uses this same term to describe creation in his sermon on Mars Hill:

> The God who made the world [*cosmos*] and everything in it, being Lord of heaven and earth, does not live in temples made by man.

The Holy Spirit of God formed the *cosmos*, an ordered arrangement of heaven and earth such that creation displayed his own orderliness. This is why God declares his creation "good" (Gn 1:4, 10, 12, 18, 21, 25). The Hebrew word implies more than just moral goodness; the term embodies the idea of aesthetic beauty and harmony. Creation is beautiful because it reflects the order and harmony of God himself. Abraham Kuyper poignantly describes this characteristic work of the Spirit, "by which the formless took form, the hidden life emerged, and the things created were led to their destiny."[6]

---

[5] Graham A. Cole, *He Who Gives Life: The Doctrine of the Holy Spirit* (Wheaton: Crossway, 2007), 282.

[6] Kuyper, *The Work of the Holy Spirit*, 30.

Psalm 104 poetically embodies this idea of creation manifesting the beauty and order of God:

Bless the Lord, O my soul!
    O Lord my God, you are very great!
You are clothed with splendor and majesty,
    2 covering yourself with light as with a garment,
    stretching out the heavens like a tent.
3 He lays the beams of his chambers on the waters;
he makes the clouds his chariot;
    he rides on the wings of the wind.

The psalm proceeds by listing all of the wondrous things God has created, bursting forth with the response,

24 O LORD, how manifold are your works!
    In wisdom have you made them all;
    the earth is full of your creatures.
25 Here is the sea, great and wide,
    which teems with creatures innumerable,
    living things both small and great.

And the psalmist identifies the person of the Trinity who brings about such wondrous creation:

30 When you send forth your Spirit [rûach], they are
        created,
    and you renew the face of the ground.

Ambrose of Milan beautifully articulates the significance of the Holy Spirit's work of creation from this Psalm:

> So when the Spirit was moving upon the water, the creation was without grace; but after this world being created underwent the operation of the Spirit, it gained all the beauty of that grace, wherewith the world is illuminated. And that the grace of the universe cannot abide without the Holy Spirit the prophet declared when he said: "Thou wilt take away thy Spirit, and they will fail and be turned again into their dust. Send forth thy Spirit, and they shall be made, and thou wilt renew all the face of the earth." Not only, then, did he teach that no creature can stand without the Holy Spirit, but also that the Spirit is the Creator of the whole creation.[7]

The Holy Spirit of God, in his active work of creation, brought wondrous order to the world that God made.

---

[7] Ambrose of Milan, "Three Books of St. Ambrose on the Holy Spirit," in *St. Ambrose: Select Works and Letters*, ed. Philip Schaff and Henry Wace, trans. H. de Romestin, E. de Romestin, and H. T. F. Duckworth, vol. 10, *A Select Library of the Nicene and Post-Nicene Fathers of the Christian Church, Second Series* (New York: Christian Literature Company, 1896), 118–119.

Wisdom and Beauty

Notice also the particular quality that characterizes the Spirit's work of creation in Psalm 104:24:

> O Lord, how manifold are your works!
> In *wisdom* have you made them all;
> the earth is full of your creatures.

Wisdom is the quality the psalmist ties to the Spirit's creative work, and this helps us to further confirm the nature of this first work of the Spirit. Wisdom is the capacity to fit things together as they ought to be, the skill to create harmony and order. Thus we should not be surprised when Proverbs 3:19 states that the Lord founded the earth by *wisdom*—by the skill to fit things together in a harmonious fashion.

This harmony and order of creation that was brought about by the Spirit of God is what we call *beauty*. Beauty is fittingness, order, and harmony. This is ultimately the Holy Spirit's work in creation. As Ambrose stated above, "After this world being created underwent the operation of the Spirit, it gained all the beauty of that grace, wherewith the world is illuminated." The Holy Spirit is the *beautifier*.

Ferguson notes that this very first action of the Holy Spirit in Scripture is "that of extending God's presence into creation in such a way as *to order and complete what has been planned in the mind of God.*[8] Jonathan Edwards developed this theme in his discussion of the Holy Spirit's work in creation:

> It was more especially the Holy Spirit's work to bring the world to its beauty and perfection out of the chaos, for the beauty of the world is a communication of God's beauty. The Holy Spirit is the harmony and excellency and beauty of the Deity . . . therefore it was his work to communicate beauty and harmony to the world, and so we read that it was he that moved upon the face of the waters.[9]

"This," Ferguson continues, "is exactly the role the Spirit characteristically fulfills elsewhere in Scripture."[10]

In other words, the Spirit's first act reveals his characteristic role within the godhead: the Holy Spirit is the divine person who orders and completes the divine plan in the created order. As we have noted, creation is one undivided act of the undivided God; all three persons of the godhead were active in creation. However, the Spirit in particular *completes* creation. As Gregory of Nyssa notes, "Every

---

[8] Ferguson, *The Holy Spirit*, 21. Emphasis original.

[9] Jonathan Edwards, "Miscellanies," no. 293, in *Works of Jonathan Edwards, 13, The "Miscellanies," (Entry Nos. a–500)*, ed. Thomas A. Schafer (New Haven, CT: Yale University Press, 1996), 384.

[10] Ferguson, *The Holy Spirit*, 21.

operation which extends from God to the Creation . . . has its origin from the Father, and proceeds through the Son, *and is perfected in the Holy Spirit*."[11] Or as Basil of Caesarea says, the Father is the "original cause," the Son is the "creative cause," and the Spirit is the "perfecting cause" of creation.[12]

Perfecting, completing, beautifying—these are the nature of the Holy Spirit's work.

Creation of the Tabernacle

In fact, the Spirit of God's creative work in Genesis 1 parallels another work of creation and beautification in Scripture—the creation of the tabernacle. Note what God says concerning the tabernacle artisans:

And you shall make holy garments for Aaron your brother, for glory and for beauty. [3] You shall speak to all the skillful, whom I have filled with a spirit [*rûach*] of

---

[11] Gregory of Nyssa, "On 'Not Three Gods,'" in *Gregory of Nyssa: Dogmatic Treatises, Etc.*, ed. Philip Schaff and Henry Wace, trans. Henry Austin Wilson, vol. 5, A Select Library of the Nicene and Post-Nicene Fathers of the Christian Church, Second Series (New York: Christian Literature Company, 1893), 334.

[12] Basil of Caesarea, *The Book of Saint Basil on the Spirit*, NPNF 2, 8:23.

skill, that they make Aaron's garments to consecrate him for my priesthood. (Ex 28:2-3)

Interestingly, the term translated "skill" is the Hebrew word for *wisdom*, the same virtue that characterizes God's work of creation attributed to the Spirit. In order that the artisans might be able to design beautiful garments for Aaron, God filled them with a spirit [*rûach*]—same Hebrew word that refers to the Holy Spirit—of wisdom—the capacity to create beauty and order.

Later, the connection between beauty, wisdom, and the Spirit of God is made even more explicit when God describes those who would build the tabernacle itself:

The Lord said to Moses, [2] "See, I have called by name Bezalel the son of Uri, son of Hur, of the tribe of Judah, [3] and I have filled him with the Spirit [*rûach*] of God, with ability and intelligence, with knowledge and all craftsmanship, [4] to devise artistic designs, to work in gold, silver, and bronze, [5] in cutting stones for setting, and in carving wood, to work in every craft. [6] And behold, I have appointed with him Oholiab, the son of Ahisamach, of the tribe of Dan. And I have given to all able men ability, that they may make all that I have commanded you. (Ex 31:1-6)

The Hebrew word translated "ability" in this passage is the same term translated "skill" in Exodus 28 and translated "wisdom" in Psalm 104:24 and Proverbs 3:19. Notice its close association with "craftsmanship to devise artistic designs." And most significantly for our discussion, notice how God endowed Bezalel (and Oholiab) with such ability to make the beautiful tabernacle with all of its elements: "I have filled him with the Spirit of God."

As the divine person who characteristically brings beauty and order to God's creation, the Spirit also enables humans to do the same. Ferguson observes,

> The beauty and symmetry of the work accomplished by these men in the construction of the tabernacle not only gave aesthetic pleasure, but a physical pattern in the heart of the camp which served to re-establish concrete expressions of the order and glory of the Creator and his intentions for his creation.[13]

Indeed, in his fascinating book, *Spirit and Beauty*, Patrick Sherry demonstrates that "a long list of Christian theologians, from Irenaeus and Clement of Alexandria in the early Church to more recent writers like Edwards and Evdokimov, have associated the Holy Spirit with beauty."[14] The Holy Spirit's work of beautifying could be considered a subset of the broader category of ordering.

---

[13] Ferguson, *The Holy Spirit*, 22.

[14] Patrick Sherry, *Spirit and Beauty: An Introduction to Theological Aesthetics*, Second edition (Scm Press, 2002), 77.

One other biblical example drives home this characteristic work of the Holy Spirit to bring order out of chaos. Isaiah 32 comes in the midst of a series of "woe" oracles that pronounce judgment upon the people of Israel. Yet chapter 32 promises a day when such judgment will be reversed at the coming of Messiah's kingdom. One way the prophet describes such a day is with a contrast between judgment and blessing. He states that Jerusalem "will be deserted . . . until the Spirit [*rûach*] is poured upon us from on high, and the wilderness becomes a fruitful field, and the fruitful field is counted as a forest" (Is 32:14–15, NKJV). The Spirit of God is the one who comes to turn judgment and desolation into fruitfulness and beauty.[15] He turns what is disordered and ugly into order and beauty.

Creation of Human Life

The Spirit of God was instrumental in bringing harmony and beauty to all creation at the beginning of time, and he had a particularly significant part in the unique creation of human life. Genesis 2:7 states,

---

[15] It is significant that Peter quotes similar language about the pouring out of the Spirit from Joel 2 when he describes what is happening on the day of Pentecost (Acts 2:17–21). This should weigh heavily in any interpretation of the Holy Spirit's unique work in this age. See chapter 8.

> Then the Lord God formed the man of dust from the ground and breathed into his nostrils the breath of life, and the man became a living creature.

"Breath" here is a different term than the one translated "Spirit" [rûach] in 1:2; however, the two terms are often used in parallel senses, indicating an intentional connection between "breath" and the Holy Spirit. For example, Job 27:3 employs both terms in a parallel fashion when it states, "as long as my *breath* is in me, and the *spirit* [rûach] of God is in my nostrils." And even more significantly, Job 33:4 uses both terms with direct reference to the creation of man:

> The *Spirit* [rûach] of God has made me,
> and the *breath* of the Almighty gives me life.

The Spirit of God *is* the breath of the almighty that gives life to every man, that creates harmonious life in what would otherwise be lifeless clay. By the power of the Spirit, man was uniquely given a spirit, unlike anything else in God's creation.

This, too, was a means by which the Spirit brought God's eternal plan to create a people for his name's sake. Isaiah 43:7 states that God made man for his own glory, and the Spirit brought that purpose to completion in creating life in Adam.

The Virgin Conception

The Spirit of God was also instrumental in creating another human life—the Last Adam, Jesus Christ. The conception of the Messiah was accomplished not through the union of a man and a woman; rather, Mary "was found to be
with child from the Holy Spirit" (Mt 1:18, 20). Gabriel had
announced to Mary that "the Holy Spirit will come upon
you, and the power of the Most High will overshadow you;
therefore the child to be born will be called holy—the Son
of God" (Lk 1:35). As he had done with the original creation,
the Spirit took what had already been created by God
(Mary's body) "in order to produce the 'second man' and
through him restore true order, just as he brought order
and fullness into the formlessness and emptiness of the
original creation."[16]

Understanding these two significant works of bringing
life and order to creation in both the First Adam and the
Last Adam helps us to recognize a foundational truth as we
consider the Holy Spirit's characteristic work: what the
Spirit does is never for its own sake or performed independently of the purposes of God. Every work of the Spirit
serves God's eternal plan for his world and his people. In
ordering God's creation, beautifying Israel's tabernacle,

---

[16] Ferguson, *The Holy Spirit*, 39.

and bringing life to the First Adam and the Last Adam, the Spirit perfects and completes God's eternal plan in history.

Live in Harmony with the Spirit

Since the Holy Spirit of God is the great Beautifier who brings all of God's world into harmony with God's nature and purposes, we Christians have the responsibility to live in harmony with the beauty of God. This is what Paul prays for in Philippians 1:

> And it is my prayer that your love may abound more and more, with knowledge and all discernment, [10] so that you may approve what is excellent, and so be pure and blameless for the day of Christ, [11] filled with the fruit of righteousness that comes through Jesus Christ, to the glory and praise of God. (Phil 1:9-11)

What Paul prays for here is a rightly ordered love—love characterized by full knowledge of God and his Word. Ordinate love is not in the eye of the beholder; it is not love for whatever I happen to consider lovely. No, rightly-ordered love is delighting in that those things that *are* lovely. God commands us to "prove all things; hold fast to that which is good" (1 Thes 5:21). The term "good" there is the same term used in the Greek translation of "good" in Genesis 1, a word that embodies the ideas of harmony and order. Likewise, Paul commands us to "think on" those things that are objectively lovely and *worthy* of our delight (Phil 4:8). In each of these passages we are called to test what we perceive and then delight in those things that are worthy of delight based on how they compare to the objective qualities of order and harmony inherent to God's nature and manifested in his creation.

This is made clear by the second term Paul uses to describe ordinate love in Philippians 1:9—discernment, a translation of the Greek word *aisthēsis,* the source of our English word *aesthetics* and a term that refers to the biblical virtue of wisdom. As we have seen, wisdom is the ability to take all of the knowledge you have gleaned about God and his world and then discern how other elements *fit* into the larger whole, whether they be ways of life, personal experiences, events happening around us—wisdom (discernment/*aisthēsis*) is the capacity to discern what *fits* in God's design for the world and what does not fit.

The cultivation of knowledge *and* discernment ought to be the aim of the Christian life. Many Christians accumulate a lot of knowledge, but relatively few truly have the capacity to perceive how that knowledge fits together harmoniously so that, as Paul continues in Philippians 1:10, we "may approve things that are excellent." Biblical discernment is the capacity to approve what is truly excellent—what is truly beautiful.

As we will continue to see, this is what the Spirit of God cultivates within his people, bringing them into harmony with his nature and purposes.

4

Revelation

While creation is the Holy Spirit's first act in Scripture, the overwhelmingly dominant work attributed to the Spirit in both Testaments is the giving of revelation.

Thus Says the Lord

Scripture frequently attributes direct revelation from God given to prophets to the person of the Holy Spirit. Joseph was able to interpret Pharaoh's dreams because the Spirit of God was in him (Gn 41:38). Saul and his messengers were able to prophesy when "the Spirit of God came upon" them (1 Sm 19:20, 23). David's last words were a prophecy, and notice who he credits for the revelation:

The oracle of David, the son of Jesse,
  the oracle of the man who was raised on high,
the anointed of the God of Jacob,
  the sweet psalmist of Israel:

[2] *"The Spirit of the Lord speaks by me;*
  his word is on my tongue.

³ The God of Israel has spoken;

the Rock of Israel has said to me:

When one rules justly over men,

ruling in the fear of God,

⁴ he dawns on them like the morning light,

like the sun shining forth on a cloudless morning,

like rain that makes grass to sprout from the earth.

(2 Sm 23:1-4)

In fact, the New Testament explicitly attributes David's revelation to the Spirit (Mt 22:43). The Spirit spoke through Zedekiah (2 Chr 18:23), Micaiah (1 Kgs 22:24), Amasai (1 Chr 12:18), Zechariah (2 Chr 24:20), Ezekiel (Ez 2:2), and Micah (Mi 3:8). The preponderance of attribution to the Spirit of God's revelation could lead us to assume that all divine revelation came by means of the Holy Spirit.

In the New Testament we see the same sort of attribution. The Spirit spoke to Jesus himself (Mt 4:1), and he promised his disciples that the Spirit would speak through them:

But the Helper, the Holy Spirit, whom the Father will send in my name, *he will teach you all things* and bring to your remembrance all that I have said to you. (Jn 14:26; cf. Mt 10:20, Lk 12:12)

Later, apostolic revelation is explicitly attributed to the Holy Spirit:

In the first book, O Theophilus, I have dealt with all that Jesus began to do and teach, [2] until the day when he was taken up, after *he had given commands through the Holy Spirit to the apostles* whom he had chosen. (Acts 1:1-2; cf. Eph 3:5)

The Spirit spoke through Elizabeth (Lk 1:41), Zechariah (Lk 1:67), Simeon (Lk 2:26), Stephen (Acts 6:8), Philip (Acts 8:29), Peter (Acts 10:19), Agabus (Acts 11:28), Paul (Acts 13:2, 20:23, 21:11, 1 Cor 2:13), and leaders of the Jerusalem council (Acts 15:28). The Spirit also "came on" the first Gentiles who were converted outside Israel, causing them to prophesy, as confirmation that they, too, were added to Christ's body (Acts 19:6). And the Spirit gave revelation to others during the foundational years of the church before God's revelation had been inscripturated in the completed canon of Scripture (Acts 21:4, 1 Cor 14).

Prophets like Isaiah and Jeremiah epitomize the nature of biblical prophecy. God told Jeremiah, "Behold, I have put my words in your mouth" (Jer 1:9). Since the Spirit is God, the revelation he gives is God's words. Isaiah, too, is told that God's words are in his mouth, and this giving of divine revelation is specifically attributed to God's Spirit "who is on you" (Is 59:12). God had characterized Moses as a prophet in a similar way, and in promising a Messianic prophet who would follow in the tradition of the Old

Testament prophets of old, God emphasized the authoritative nature of such prophecy:

> I will raise up for them a prophet like you from among their brothers. And I will put my words in his mouth, and he shall speak to them all that I command him. [19] And whoever will not listen to my words that he shall speak in my name, I myself will require it of him. (Dt 18:18-19)

Because of the divine weight of such prophecy, those who claimed to be prophets had to be tested, and any who failed the test would be killed since he was falsely claiming to speak the very words of God (Dt 13:1-5, 18:15-22). Paul commanded the same standard of testing prophecy in the New Testament (1 Cor 14:29).

To prophesy is to speak the very words of God. Sometimes those words are predictive; more often those words are instructive or exhortative. But no matter the content, prophecy is the delivery of direct, divine revelation from the Spirit of God to the degree that one who prophesies can always unequivocally say, "Thus says the Lord."

I mentioned in chapter 1 that moderate charismatics like Wayne Grudem teach that NT prophecy takes a different form than the standard of OT prophecy. He states,

> Prophecy in ordinary New Testament churches was not equal to Scripture in authority but was simply a very

human—and sometimes partially mistaken—report of something the Holy Spirit brought to someone's mind.[1]

However, as Bruce Compton convincingly argues, "Grudem has failed to make his case for New Testament prophecy that is errant and lacking in divine authority." Compton demonstrates that "the evidence speaks unequivocally in support of the inerrancy and authority of New Testament prophecy." Thus, Grudem and other evangelical continuationists can't have it both ways: "If New Testament prophecy is ongoing, then the canon cannot be closed. Or, if the canon is closed, then there can be no continuing New Testament prophecy."[2]

God-Breathed

Similar to his work of creation, Spirit-given revelation had the ultimate purpose of bringing order to God's plan in the world. The Holy Spirit gave special revelation to disclose the nature and character of God, explain God's requirements, correct sin, and give hope for the future. In fact, based on the fact that the giving of revelation is the most repeated work of the Spirit in both Testaments, it is

---

[1] Grudem, *The Gift of Prophecy in the New Testament and Today*, 18.

[2] Bruce Compton, "The Continuation of New Testament Prophecy and a Closed Canon: Revisiting Wayne Grudem's Two Levels of NT Prophecy," *Detroit Baptist Seminary Journal* 22 (2017): 71.

safe to say that the primary way God orders his plan in history is through Spirit-given revelation. At each major stage in the progress of God's plan, the Spirit of God revealed the truth necessary for God's people to be blessed.

But ultimately, the Holy Spirit inspired a "prophetic word more fully confirmed" (2 Pt 1:19-21), the canonical Scriptures that are "breathed out by God" and given to believers "for teaching, for reproof, for correction, and for training in righteousness, that the man of God may be complete, equipped for every good work" (2 Tm 3:16-17).

The term translated "breathed out by God" is *Theopneustos; Theos* is the Greek term for "God" and *pneuma* means "breath" or "spirit." The very words of Scripture were produced by the Spirit of God as he carried along holy men of God. Every word of Scripture carries with it the weight of "Thus Says the Lord."

What the New Testament explicitly teaches regarding divine inspiration was already implicitly taught in the Old Testament. For example, when God told Isaiah that his Spirit would put words in his mouth, he declared that those words would "not depart out of your mouth, or out of the mouth of your offspring, or out of the mouth of your children's offspring . . . from this time forth and forevermore" (Is 59:21).

The nature of such inspiration is important as well: the Holy Spirit did not inspire the Scriptures by bringing authors into a sort of mystical trance as they were "carried along" (2 Pt 1:21); rather, as helpfully defined by John Frame, inspiration is "a divine act that creates an identity between a divine word and a human word"[3]—each author conscientiously penned the Scriptures (Acts 1:16, 4:25, Heb 3:7, 1 Cor 2:12-13) using craftsmanship (e.g. the Psalms), research (e.g. Lk 1:1-4), and available cultural forms and idioms.

In other words, Spirit-inspired revelation is both for the purpose of order and produced in an orderly fashion.

The More Sure Word

In understanding the nature of the Spirit's work of giving revelation, it is important that we understand the relationship between the revelation that he gave directly through prophets and the revelation that he inspired in the sixty-six canonical books of Scripture. While both oral revelation and written revelation are authoritative revelation from the Spirit of God, only written revelation is described as "God-breathed." Unlike oral revelation, which is temporary and only authoritative for those to whom it was given,

---

[3] John M. Frame, *The Doctrine of the Word of God*, vol. 4 (Phillipsburg, NJ: P&R, 2010), 140.

written revelation is permanent, preserved, and authoritative for all people in all time.[4]

Peter addresses this very issue in 2 Peter 1, where he states in verse 21, "men spoke from God as they were carried along by the Holy Spirit." Peter is discussing the nature of Spirit-inspired biblical revelation because of the false teachers who had emerged, some of whom claimed to speak for God.

Peter begins his argument, however, by appealing to his eyewitness status as an apostle of Jesus Christ—"we were eyewitnesses of his majesty." When he made known to the people truth about Jesus Christ, Peter argues, he did not follow cleverly devised myths; rather, his teaching is based on what he personally witnessed as an apostle of Christ.

To what is he referring in these verses? He is referring to the supernatural experience of the transfiguration of Jesus Christ in the presence of Peter, James, and John on the mountain. After Jesus was transfigured before them, Moses and Elijah appeared, two representatives of God's Spirit-given revelation. Then "a cloud overshadowed them" (Mk 9:7), which is likely a manifestation of the Holy Spirit. The same sort of cloud appeared when God gave his revelation from Mt. Sinai (Ex 24:15-16) and over the tabernacle (Ex

---

[4] Of course, much oral revelation was also later inspired and inscripturated, and thus became permanently preserved for all time, but other oral revelation that was not inscripturated was temporary.

40:35), and the exact same term for "overshadowed" is what Gabriel tells Mary would cause the conception of Jesus by the Spirit (Lk 1:35; cf. Mt 17:15, Lk 9:34). And out of the cloud, God the Father proclaimed, "This is my beloved Son; listen to him." The whole point of the transfiguration is the divine revelation of Christ as the Son of God.

However, notice what Peter says next in verse 19: "And we have the prophetic Word more fully confirmed." Despite all of Peter's own experiences of receiving divine revelation from God himself, Peter identifies the foundational source of God's truth: the prophetic Word. This phrase, "the prophetic Word" is normally used to describe the 39 books of the Old Testament. Peter is saying that God revealed his truth, not only through direct divine revelation, but fundamentally through his Spirit-inscripturated Word.

Peter and the other apostles did experience direct, first-hand revelation from God's Spirit. Those supernatural experiences were truly ways in which God confirmed his truth to his apostles. And yet, as Peter is trying to defend God's truth, someone could very easily say, "Why should we take your word for it? People experience things they can't explain all the time; who's to say that such experiences are direct revelation from God?" Peter answers that natural objection by saying, "Don't take my word for it. Trust the sufficient Word of God."

In fact, he goes even beyond that. The verse literally reads, "And we have *more sure* the prophetic Word." Do you see what Peter is saying here? Here is an apostle of Jesus Christ, one who walked with Jesus and saw his miracles and heard his teaching, one who performed signs of a true apostle, one of only three who saw Jesus transfigured on the mountain and literally heard the voice of God from heaven, and despite all of those amazing supernatural experiences, Peter says, "We have a prophetic Word even more certain, more confirmed, more sure than those supernatural experiences. We have the written Word of God, *and that Word is sufficient.*"

Often Christians today assume that if the Spirit of God spoke directly to them like he did to prophets and apostles in Scripture, they would far more easily align their lives with God's will for them. But Peter is saying that the Spirit-inspired Word is more certain than if the Spirit spoke directly to us.

Consider what he says in the next phrase in verse 19: "to which you would do well to pay attention." Pay attention to the sufficient Word. We ought not to expect the Spirit to speak directly to us, because even if he did, the Word would still be more sure than that direct revelation from the Spirit. Why would we want something *less sure* than the Word of God?

In fact, the reason we even know about the transfiguration (or any other truth about Christ) is not that the Spirit directly revealed it to us, and not even because Peter or another apostle told us directly. The only reason we have this truth is that the Spirit inscripturated that revelation in the written Word.

In fact, when Peter says in verse 16, "we *made known* to you the power and coming of our Lord Jesus Christ," that phrase "made known" is a technical word that refers to imparting new divine revelation (cf. Lk 2:15). Peter's teaching and even the account of the transfiguration were God's revelation to his apostles that was then written as inspired Scripture.

This act of inspiration is what the apostle Paul is referring to in 1 Corinthians 2:10–13, a text sometimes used to claim that the Spirit speaks directly to everyone:

> These things God has revealed to us through the Spirit. For the Spirit searches everything, even the depths of God. [11] For who knows a person's thoughts except the spirit of that person, which is in him? So also no one comprehends the thoughts of God except the Spirit of God. [12] Now we have received not the spirit of the world, but the Spirit who is from God, that we might understand the things freely given us by God. [13] And we impart this in words not taught by human wisdom but taught by the Spirit, interpreting spiritual truths to those who are spiritual.

Two points are important to recognize in this text: First, the "us" and "we" in verses 10–13 are the apostles and other authors of Scripture. Charles Hodge notes, "The whole connection shows that the apostle is speaking of revelation and inspiration; and therefore *we* must mean *we apostles*, (or Paul himself), and not we Christians."[5] These men certainly received direct revelation from the Spirit of God so that whatever they wrote can be considered "inspired" by God (2 Tm 3:16; 2 Pt 20-21). But we must remember that such inspiration was unique. The Spirit uniquely revealed the truths of Scripture to these men, and these truths are now inscripturated in the sixty-six canonical books of Scripture. The Spirit does not "reveal" truth to us in the same manner. These verses describe *inspiration of Scripture*.

This is important to remember in any discussion of the Spirit's revelation: the primary way the Spirit brings God's Word to us is not through direct revelation; rather, God's Spirit has already brought God's Word to us perfectly and sufficiently through *inspiration*.

Peter summarizes this very point in chapter 3:

> This is now the second letter that I am writing to you, beloved. In both of them I am stirring up your sincere mind by way of reminder, [2] that you should remember the predictions of the holy prophets [that's the OT] and the commandment of the Lord and Savior through your apostles [that's the NT]. (2 Pt 3:1-2)

---

[5] Charles Hodge, *An Exposition of the First Epistle to the Corinthians* (New York: Robert Carter & Brothers, 1860), 40. Emphasis original.

Not all of the New Testament had been completed at this point, of course, but Peter and the other apostles knew what they were writing. In fact, later in chapter 3, Peter refers to Paul's letters as Scripture (3:15-16). In 1 Timothy 5:18, Paul refers to Luke's writings as Scripture. Paul calls his own writings "a command of the Lord" (1 Cor 14:37-38) and "the Word of God" (1 Thes 2:13). They knew they were writing a more sure prophetic Word.

There are those today who insist that nowhere does Scripture say that the Spirit has stopped giving direct revelation now that Scripture is complete, but that is exactly what Peter is saying here. The written Word of God is *more sure* than direct revelation; direct revelation was only necessary for a time because the more sure written Word was not yet complete. Now that the written Word *is* complete, we no longer need those *less sure* revelations.

The only reason to believe that God's Spirit still speaks through divine revelation is if you believe the canon of Scripture is incomplete; if you believe that the canon of Scripture is closed, then you ought not expect any additional divine revelation. Even Grudem acknowledges, "If everyone with the gift of prophecy in the New Testament church did have . . . absolute divine authority, then we would expect this gift to die out as soon as the writings of the New Testament were completed and given to the churches."[6] John Owen famously observed, if "private revelations agree with Scripture, they are needless, and if they disagree, they are false."[7]

As I noted in chapter 1, many people today think that supernatural experiences were just the normal, expected way God spoke to everyone in biblical times. But this reveals two misconceptions about the examples of direct revelation that are recorded for us in Scripture.

First, direct revelation from the Spirit was rare in biblical history. People assume they happened all the time, but really, they occurred mostly in only three general periods: the patriarchs and Moses, Elijah and the prophets, Jesus and the founding of the church by his apostles. There are large spans of history between those three primary periods where hearing from God's Spirit outside of his Word was not the normal experience.

Even in Acts, the normal expectation was *not* to expect direct revelation from God, but to trust his sufficient Word. Direct revelations occur only nine separate times over the course of thirty years in the Book of Acts. On the other hand, there are at least 70 instances in Acts where Christians, including the apostles, made decisions without direct revelation.

---

[6] Grudem, *The Gift of Prophecy in the New Testament and Today*, 45–46.

[7] Quoted from a Latin work in J. I. Packer, *A Quest for Godliness: The Puritan Vision of the Christian Life* (Wheaton, IL: Crossway, 2010), 86.

When the apostles were choosing a replacement for Judas, they did not ask for direct revelation—they consulted the Word, and then made an informed decision. When they chose the first deacons, appointed elders, decided where to preach the gospel, and even at the Jerusalem Counsel, God's people made important decisions, not on the basis of direct revelation or impressions from the Holy Spirit, but on the basis of careful application of the sufficient Word. Direct revelation was not a regular occurrence even for the apostles in the first century.

Second, people misunderstand the purpose of those instances of direct revelation. Those experiences did not exist for their own sake as the normal way God revealed his will to his people. Rather, those times when the Spirit spoke directly through prophets were for the purpose of *confirming* the written Word of God as it was being given as the more sure Word, and once the written Word was confirmed, direct revelation was no longer necessary.

Think about those three periods of history: God spoke directly to the people through Moses, but then God *wrote* his revelation in the tablets of stone and in his *written* Word. The direct revelation *confirmed* that the law and the testimony was from God, but once it was written, God didn't speak directly to the people. He expected the people to trust and obey something *more sure*—his written Word. God's Word was sufficient.

The Holy Spirit spoke through the prophets like Elijah and Isaiah, but then those prophets *wrote* what God said. The direct revelation *confirmed* that the prophecy was from God, but once it was written, God didn't speak directly to the people. He expected the people to trust and obey something *more sure*—his written Word. God's Word was sufficient.

And likewise, God's Spirit spoke directly through Jesus and his apostles. But then, as Peter said in chapter 3, the apostles *wrote* what God said. The direct revelation *confirmed* that the revelation was from God, but now that it has been written, we should not expect God to speak directly to us. God expects us to trust and obey something *more sure*— his written Word. God's Word is sufficient.

It is foolish for us to look at what God was doing in those three unique periods when he was progressively delivering his revelation and assume them to be normative for us today. Those three periods when the Spirit did speak directly produced the more sure written Word of God: Moses, Elijah and the prophets, Jesus and the apostles—the Law, the Prophets, and the New Testament. And, remarkably, this is exactly who gathered together on the Mount of Transfiguration: Moses, Elijah, Jesus and his apostles—representatives of the sixty-six inspired, authoritative, inscripturated, *more sure*, sufficient Word of God, and this Word will be sufficient until Jesus comes again.

The reason that the written Word is more sure than direct revelation from the Spirit is because of the nature of inspiration. Peter addresses this in verse 20:

> Knowing this first of all, that no prophecy of Scripture comes from someone's own interpretation. For no prophecy was ever produced by the will of men.

In other words, the inscripturated Word of God does not come from a human source. If it did, Scripture would not be inerrant, infallible, authoritative, or sufficient. This is the problem with even supernatural subjective revelations—they are fallible because humans are fallible. Visions can be caused by lack of sleep, inner promptings can be indigestion, and dreams can be caused by too much spicy food. If you heard a voice from heaven, you couldn't be certain it was actually God.

But what has been written down in the Scriptures is not like this. It is not from a human source. This is what makes Scripture even more trustworthy and preferred to direct revelation from God. No prophecy of *Scripture* comes from a human source. Rather, "men spoke from God as they were carried along by the Holy Spirit" (v. 21). Peter is saying that we ought to trust the sufficient Word because it is revelation from God's Spirit that is even more sure than if he spoke to us directly.

The Profitable Word

The key text on the inspiration of Scripture, 2 Timothy 3:16–17, confirms that the purpose of Spirit-given Scripture is to order our lives:

> All Scripture is breathed out by God and profitable for teaching, for reproof, for correction, and for training in righteousness, that the man of God may be complete, equipped for every good work.

Because Scripture is God-breathed, Spirit-produced Scripture is profitable and sufficient to make us "complete, equipped for every good work." The word translated "complete" and the word translated "equipped" are actually different forms of the same term that communicate the idea of being perfectly adapted for a task. This significant work of the Spirit of God to produce sixty-six inerrant, infallible books of inscripturated revelation is sufficient for every remaining activity the Spirit's work to bring order to God's plan and people.

In other words, as we continue to work through other works of the Holy Spirit, what we will notice is that the Holy Spirit's active work today is all done *through* the sufficient Word that he inspired. The Holy Spirit regenerates dead hearts through his sufficient Word. The Holy Spirit illuminates blind hearts, causing believers to accept the sufficient Word as the true words of God. The Holy Spirit convicts us of sin through his sufficient Word. He sanctifies us through his sufficient Word. He comforts us through his sufficient Word. To be filled by the Spirit (Eph 5:19) is to let the sufficient Word of Christ richly dwell within us (Col 3:16).

Without the Holy Spirit's work, the Word would not be effectual for regeneration, sanctification, conviction, or comfort—The Holy Spirit actively works *through* the sufficient Word that he inspired to make it effectual in our hearts. And the truth is that all of these works of the Holy Spirit *are* supernatural experiences, and he accomplishes those supernatural works *through* his inspired Word.

Listen to the Holy Spirit

We ought not wonder why the Holy Spirit isn't speaking to us any more today. Rather, we must recognize that the Spirit of God has already spoken to us *and continues to do so* through his sufficient Word—we ought not expect any further revelation or even impressions. We must simply pray that the Spirit will give us wisdom to appropriate his Word and then actively apply it and submit ourselves to what he has already spoken.

Trust the sufficient Word. It's the only Spirit-given revelation we need. We do not need the voice of God from heaven, we do not need a still small voice in our hearts, we do not need visions or dreams or impressions or "nudges from the Holy Spirit"—we have something better than all of that. We have more sure the written Word of God. Scripture is sufficient.

The only day when we will no longer need the written Word of God is when the day dawns and the morning star rises in our hearts (2 Pt 1:19), when *The Word*, Jesus Christ, comes again in all of his glory, when we will see him face to face, when faith will be sight. Then, and only then, will we have something more sure than the written Word of God.

5

Empowerment

As we saw in the last chapter, one of the Holy Spirit's primary works has been to give revelation to key leaders of God's people in the progress of God's redemptive history, culminating in Holy Scripture, which was written by men who were carried along by the Holy Spirit.

But the Holy Spirit also gave some of these same leaders special empowerment in addition to direct revelation. For example, the Old Testament describes the Holy Spirit being "upon" Moses and the elders of Israel, Joshua, judges such as Gideon and Samson, and prophets such as Elijah and Micah. He also uniquely came upon Israel's kings, Saul and David.

Theocratic Anointing

This Spirit empowerment gave individuals a variety of special abilities primarily so that they could lead God's people. This is why such special empowerment is sometimes called "theocratic anointing." In fact, as we noted in the last chapter, often the prophecy itself was given as a sign that these individuals were chosen and empowered by the Spirit for such leadership. For example, as ruler of Israel (Acts 7:35), Moses had a special anointing of the Spirit (Nm 11:17). God confirmed that anointing in the sight of the people through the miracle of changing Moses's staff into a snake (Ex 40:30–31). Later, Moses "took some of the Spirit that was on him and put it on the seventy elders. And as soon as the Spirit rested on them, they prophesied. But they did not continue doing it" (Nm 11:25). The special empowerment by the Spirit was so that the elders could "bear some of the burden of the people" as rulers alongside Moses, and they prophesied as confirmation that they were to share the burden of leadership.

That leadership passed on to Joshua as Moses's successor, who then is described as "full of the Spirit of wisdom, for Moses had laid his hands on him" (Dt 34:9). God specifically told Joshua, "Just as I was with Moses, so I will be with you" (Jo 1:56). And God confirmed Joshua's leadership of the people with the crossing of the Jordan river on dry ground (Jo 4), a supernatural miracle that would have immediately brought to mind Moses's miracle of crossing the Red Sea (Ex 14:31). The result was that Joshua was confirmed as ruler of the people: "On that day the Lord exalted Joshua in the sight of all Israel, and they stood in awe of him just as they had stood in awe of Moses, all the days of his life" (Jo 4:14).

Four judges of Israel are described as having this special Spirit anointing: Othniel (Jgs 3:10), Gideon (Jgs 6:34), Jepthah (Jgs 11:29), and Samson (Jgs 15:14). It is not a stretch to assume that this theocratic anointing came upon all of the judges whom God appointed as leaders of his people.

When leadership of Israel moved to a monarchy, so did the theocratic anointing of the Spirit. After Samuel anointed Saul as king of Israel (1 Sm 10:1), "the Spirit of God rushed upon him, and he prophesied among them" (1 Sm 10:10). The same happened later to David: "Then Samuel took the horn of oil and anointed him in the midst of his brothers. And the Spirit of the Lord rushed upon David from that day forward" (1 Sm 16:13). Likewise, Solomon's prayer for wisdom was, in effect, a request for the same special empowerment from the Spirit (1 Kgs 3:9). The first result of the empowerment given to him by the Spirit was his ability to wisely judge the case of the two women fighting over the death of one of their babies. This exercise of divine empowerment confirmed Solomon as leader of God's people: "And all Israel heard of the judgment that the king had rendered, and they stood in awe of the king, because they perceived that the wisdom of God was in him to do justice" (1 Kgs 3:28).

Prophets, too, appear to have had a special empowerment from the Spirit, though perhaps this would not necessarily be called theocratic anointing since they were not rulers. Yet the purpose of such empowerment was similar:

to confirm them as messengers of God. For example, the Spirit was known to carry Elijah to places unknown (1 Kgs 18:12), and Micah declared of himself, "I am filled with power, with the Spirit of the Lord, and with justice and might" (Mic 3:8). Indeed, as we have already noted, Spirit empowerment and direct divine revelation went hand in hand.

So this empowerment was primarily given by the Spirit to equip leaders of God's people, often resulting in unique wisdom, physical strength, and revelation from God, to bring God's people into order with God's plan and purposes. And the miraculous works performed by these individuals as a result of the Spirit's anointing were for the purpose of confirming them as rulers and messengers of God in the sight of the people.

This act of the Holy Spirit was never permanent. The Spirit left Samson after Delilah cut his hair, for example, causing him to lose his special strength (Jgs 16:20). The most notable illustration of this is when "the Spirit of the Lord departed from Saul" after his sin (1 Sm 16:14). Just prior to that, Samuel had anointed David as the new king of Israel, "and the Spirit of the Lord rushed upon David from that day forward" (1 Sm 16:13). This also explains why David prayed that God would not take his Holy Spirit from him after his sin with Bathsheba (Ps 51:11). David wasn't afraid that he would lose the indwelling presence of God's Spirit that brings salvation—once we are saved, we never lose the

Spirit in that sense (Eph 1:13–14). Rather, what David feared was that the Spirit would remove his special anointing empowerment given to him as king of Israel.

This special Spirit empowerment was even applied to non-believers on occasion. King Saul is, of course, an example of this. Though God anointed him as king of Israel and gifted him with special empowerment from the Spirit, his actions revealed that he was not a true follower of Yahweh. Likewise "the Spirit of God came upon" Balaam and caused him to bless Israel, though Balaam's desire was to curse Israel (Nm 24:2).

What is clear, then, is that this empowerment by the Spirit is not related to other works by the Spirit that are given to all believers. This empowerment is unique gifting by the Spirit to leaders of God's people and prophets in order that he might work his plan among them. Alva J. McClain says of this special Spirit-empowerment,

> Three things should be noted about this coming of the Spirit upon the great leaders of the historical kingdom: first, it was not always related to high moral character; second, in certain cases its outstanding effects were seen chiefly in the realm of the purely physical; third, and most important of all, it had to do primarily with

the regal functions of those who stood as mediators of the divine government of Israel.[1]

This fact alone reveals the unique nature of Spirit empowerment—it is not intended for every believer, or even just those who are especially holy. Rather, the Spirit empowered very specific individuals who were especially chosen by God to deliver his revelation or otherwise order the people and plan of God at significant stages in redemptive history. Between those significant transitional stages, such empowerment is not ordinary or necessary.

Filled with the Spirit

Old Testament prophecy also foretells a similar empowerment given by the Spirit to the coming Messiah. Isaiah 11:2 prophesies,

> And the Spirit of the Lord shall rest upon him,
>> the Spirit of wisdom and understanding,
>> the Spirit of counsel and might,
>> the Spirit of knowledge and the fear of the Lord.

And again in Isaiah 61:1–2,

> The Spirit of the Lord God is upon me,

---

[1] Alva J. McClain, *The Greatness of the Kingdom* (Winona Lake, IL: BMH Books, 1959), 93.

because the Lord has anointed me
to bring good news to the poor;
he has sent me to bind up the brokenhearted,
to proclaim liberty to the captives,
and the opening of the prison to those who are
bound;
[2] to proclaim the year of the Lord's favor.

This is the same theocratic anointing of the Spirit given to leaders of God's people, especially kings of Israel.

Not surprisingly, then, the earliest examples of this Spirit empowerment in the NT apply specifically to Jesus Christ, first pictured when "the Holy Spirit descended on him in bodily form, like a dove," at his baptism (Lk 3:22). John the Baptist later declared that Jesus had been given "the Spirit without measure" (Jn 3:34). Notably, Jesus launched his public ministry in Nazareth when he read Isaiah's prophecy that the Spirit would anoint the Messiah and claimed to be that very Anointed One (Lk 4:16–21).

Although Jesus himself is fully divine, Jesus often attributed his power while on earth to the Holy Spirit. He was driven into the wilderness by the Spirit to be tempted (Mk 1:12), and he returned to Galilee "in the power of the Spirit" (Lk 4:14). Jesus claimed that he cast out demons "by the Spirit of God" (Mt 12:28). And Jesus declares that anyone who attributed one of his works done in the power of the Spirit to Satan "will not be forgiven" (Mt 12:31). Later, Luke describes Jesus's teaching as having been given "through the Holy Spirit" (Acts 1:2) and noted how "God anointed Jesus of Nazareth with the Holy Spirit and with power" (Acts 10:38).

The Holy Spirit also uniquely empowered other key spiritual leaders in the NT, such as John the Baptist, whom Gabriel promised would "be filled with the Holy Spirit, even from his mother's womb" (Lk 1:15). Christ's apostles, too, are described similarly. For example, on the Day of Pentecost, the apostles "were all filled with the Holy Spirit and began to speak in other tongues as the Spirit gave them utterance" (Acts 2:4). Likewise, after they experienced persecution, "they were all filled with the Holy Spirit and continued to speak the word of God with boldness" (Acts 4:31). After Saul was converted on the road to Damascus, Ananias laid hands on him, and Saul was "filled with the Holy Spirit" (Acts 9:17; cf. 13:9).

In these cases, Luke describes this special empowerment as being "filled with the Holy Spirit," but it is important to recognize the difference between this special filling and the kind of filling Paul commands in Ephesians 5:18 when he admonishes, "be filled by the Spirit."

In Luke and Acts, Luke uses the term *pimplēmi* in the passive voice, in which the grammar clearly indicates that the Holy Spirit is the *content* of the filling and that the individual filled with the Spirit does not do anything to cause it.[2] Luke uses different terms to describe the kind of filling that is true of all believers. He uses the term *plērēs* in five places and *plēroō* once to designate a more general Spirit-filling of the disciples in Acts 13:52, and this latter term is what Paul states as a command in Ephesians 5:18.[3] We will look specifically at what this more general Spirit-filling is in chapter 7. For now, it is important to recognize the distinction between the more general Spirit-filling commanded of all believers (*plērēs/plēroō*) and the Spirit-filling given to key leaders of God's people to empower them in their role (*pimplēmi*).

Ordering God's People

As we have noted, the empowering of individual leaders for special service was for the ultimate purpose of bringing to order God's redemptive plan in both Israel and the church. This is true of Moses and the elders of Israel. As Ferguson notes,

Just as the Spirit produced order and purpose out of the formless and empty primeval created "stuff" (Gn 1:2), so, when the nation was newborn but remained in danger of social chaos, the Spirit of God worked creatively

---

[2] These appear in Luke 1:15, 1:41, 1:67; Acts 2:4, 4:8, 4:31, 9:17, 13:9.

[3] See William W. Combs, "Spirit-Filling in Ephesians 5:18," *DBSJ* 19 (2014): 31–34.

to produce right government, order, and direction among the refugees from Egypt.[4]

This is true as well for his empowering of apostles in the early church, gifting them with the necessary abilities to both quickly spread the gospel message beyond Jerusalem "to the end of the earth" (Acts 1:8) and firmly establish the doctrine and practice of the early church (2 Cor 12:12, Heb 2:4). Paul clearly states in Ephesians 2:20 that the apostles and prophets, these individuals specially empowered by the Holy Spirit, served a unique function as the foundation of the church. The Spirit was ushering in a new age in God's redemptive plan. Once the church had been put in order, the Spirit no longer had reason to empower people in that way.

It is also important to recognize the inherent connection between this special Spirit empowerment and the giving of revelation we saw in the last chapter. The very same individuals who are described as the Spirit coming upon or filling them are those to whom the Spirit gave direct revelation so they could lead God's people appropriately. The same is true for gifting them with the ability to perform signs and wonders, which we will examine more closely in chapter 8.

---

[4] Ferguson, *The Holy Spirit*, 22.

In other words, while it is accurate to say that the Holy Spirit has empowered individuals in extraordinary ways, these were rare, they were specifically for key leaders of God's people, and their function was to bring God's purposes into order in human history. Sinclair Ferguson helpfully explains:

> In the Scriptures themselves, extraordinary gifts appear to be limited to a few brief periods in biblical history, in which they serve as confirmatory signs of new revelation and its ambassadors, and as a means of establishing and defending the kingdom of God in epochally significant ways. . . . Outbreaks of the miraculous sign gifts in the Old Testament were, generally speaking, limited to those periods of redemptive history in which a new stage of covenantal revelation was reached. . . . But these sign-deeds were never normative. Nor does the Old Testament suggest they should have continued unabated even throughout the redemptive-historical epoch they inaugurated. . . . Consistent with this pattern, the work of Christ and the apostles was confirmed by "signs and wonders."[5]

To focus on the relatively few cases in biblical history of extraordinary works of the Holy Spirit and draw from those a theology that assumes this to be his regular activity fails to

---

[5] Ferguson, *The Holy Spirit*, 224–25.

take into account the purpose of these works in the over-arching plan of God.

Furthermore, even the extraordinary works of the Spirit in Scripture, such as giving revelation or empowering for service, hardly resemble the kinds of extraordinary manifestations contemporary Christians have come to associate with the Holy Spirit, such as emotional euphoria or supernatural gifts of tongues or healing. Even if Christians in the present age should expect extraordinary works of the Spirit to regularly occur, what most contemporary evangelicals have come to expect does not fit the biblical pattern for how the Holy Spirit works.

Testifying of Christ

One of the fundamental problems with how many people conceive of the Spirit's work in history like special empowerment is that they focus only on individual acts, failing to recognize how each act of the Spirit functions in the larger scope of God's redemptive plan. This is why it is so important to recognize the Spirit's work as that of bringing order and completion to the plan of God. This is true of creation, revelation, and empowerment: each of these is a working out of the eternal plan of God.

Ultimately, God's plan is one of bringing himself glory through creating his kingdom on earth, ruled by man made in his image.[6] We have already seen this plan brought into order by the Spirit as he created the earthly kingdom realm for man to inhabit and rule. Since Adam failed in this kingly role, God's plan also included the sending of a Second Adam who would succeed where the First Adam failed and redeem a humanity who would rule and reign with him. We have seen also the Spirit's role in bringing order to that part of God's plan through the virgin conception of the Son of God.

The revelation given by the Spirit to particular individuals throughout history and ultimately inscripturated in the sixty-six books of the Bible was also inherently connected to this overarching purpose: through Spirit-given revelation, God established covenants with his people by which he would bring his plans to pass, he ordered Israel into a nation that would guard the covenants and produce the Messiah, and he prophesied of the coming King. And empowerment of key individuals, especially the theocratic anointing of rulers of his people, was also how the Spirit moved forward the plan of God to bring the perfect Redeemer-King. And as we have seen, this work culminated in anointing the Messiah himself and empowering his apostles to witness of him to the ends of the earth.

---

[6] See Scott Aniol, *Citizens and Exiles: Christian Faithfulness in God's Two Kingdoms* (Douglasville, GA: G3 Press, 2023).

What this summary of God's plan for history demonstrates is that the Spirit's work to bring order and completion to that plan is ultimately about testifying of the Anointed Messiah. In all that he does, from bringing harmony to the world, to unfolding God's revelation, to empowering God's leaders, the Spirit points to Christ. The Spirit does not perform his work randomly, independently of the plan of God, or in order to draw attention to himself. The Spirit's work always leads to the establishment and recognition of Christ the King over all the earth.

Jesus himself describes the Spirit's role in this way:

> I still have many things to say to you, but you cannot bear them now. [13] When the Spirit of truth comes, he will guide you into all the truth, for he will not speak on his own authority, but whatever he hears he will speak, and he will declare to you the things that are to come. [14] He will glorify me, for he will take what is mine and declare it to you. [15] All that the Father has is mine; therefore I said that he will take what is mine and declare it to you. (Jn 16:12–15)

Notice what Christ says: the Spirit will glorify *him*. The Spirit's revelation is truth that testifies to *Christ*: "This is he who came by water and blood—Jesus Christ; not by the water only but by the water and the blood. And the Spirit is the one who testifies, because the Spirit is the truth" (1 Jn 5:6).

What Christ says of the unique role of the Spirit in this age was true in the Old Testament as well. Again, all of the unique theocratic anointing moved toward the ultimate anointing of the Messianic King. Most significantly, the Scriptures he inspired testify to Christ (Jn 5:46).

And as we will explore in the remaining chapters, the Spirit's work in salvation, sanctification, gifting, and worship are all about causing his people to submit themselves to Christ as King, be conformed into Christ's image, build up his body, and worship him rightly. These works order God's chosen people into his plan for them.

God the Father has an eternal plan, God the Son accomplished the means for that plan to be fulfilled, and God the Spirit completes and perfects that plan directly in the world. Bringing harmony to creation, revealing God's plan to his people, and special empowerment of unique leaders of God's people at significant points in the outworking of that plan all involve how the Holy Spirit brings the plan of God into order.

Trust in Christ

When we truly understand the Holy Spirit's purpose in empowering individuals throughout history, it ought to lead us to one unmistakable conclusion: the Holy Spirit of God wants us to trust in Christ. Everything he has done to order God's plan through special empowerment led to *the Anointed One*, Jesus the Messiah.

The fact that the Holy Spirit empowered certain individuals in history ought *not* cause us to long for the same kind of empowerment; to do so is evidence that we misunderstand the Spirit's purpose.

Rather, trust in the One who came in the line of Spirit-anointed kings, the One Spirit-empowered prophets foretold, the One for whom the Spirit filled John the Baptist to prepare, the one of whom the apostles were empowered to witness: Jesus Christ.

6

Salvation

The works of the Spirit of God we have seen up to this point are unique in unfolding God's eternal plan in past history. The purpose of ordering the plans of God accomplished by the Spirit through creation, revelation, and special empowerment have been finished. Creation is complete, the Spirit-inspired Word is complete, and Spirit empowerment functioned at key transitional periods in the history of redemption that finished their intended purpose. Therefore, we should not expect these sorts of extraordinary works until the next stage in redemptive history—when the Anointed King comes again.

Beginning with this chapter, however, we will begin to explore ordinary activities of the Spirit that have been at work since the beginning of time and will continue until the eternal kingdom.

Scripture appropriates specific acts to each divine person of the godhead in the salvation of God's elect. The Father planned salvation and sent his Son into the world to save his people. The Son took on flesh, lived a perfect life, and died to pay the penalty of sin, accomplishing redemption for his people. And as with other aspects of God's eternal plans, the Spirit actively works *to order and complete* God's plan of salvation in the lives of his elect.

Conviction

This work begins with convicting sinners. Jesus promised that he would send the Spirit to "convict the world concerning sin and righteousness and judgment" (Jn 16:8). Without the Spirit's conviction, sinners would have no spiritual awareness of their need of salvation. Conviction is the first step in bringing sinful, disordered souls into order and harmony with God's perfect will.

Regeneration

Next, the Spirit gives new life. Jesus specifically identified the Spirit as the one who gives new birth (Jn 3:5, 8). Likewise, Paul describes him as "the Spirit of life" (Rom 8:2) and tells us in Titus 3:5 that God saved us "by the washing of regeneration and renewal of the Holy Spirit." This work of the Spirit ties directly to his very first work—creation. The regenerating work of the Spirit is his *recreation* of dead sinners into new creations (2 Cor 5:17).

Although some deny regeneration in the Old Testament, due to the fact that it is not as clearly articulated as in the New Testament, a few keys points lead to the conclusion that the Holy Spirit did regenerate Old Testament believers. First, although the Old Covenant promised life (Lev 18:5), the Law could not provide life on its own. Only through the regenerating power of the Spirit could an individual keep the Law.

Second, God promised his people in the Old Testament that God "will circumcise your heart and the heart and the heart of your offspring," which he would later promise as a work of the Spirit in the New Covenant (Jer 31:33; 32:39-40; Ezek 11:19; 36:26-27). The phrase "circumcise your heart" was a metaphor for Spirit regeneration. Likewise, the psalmist prays, "incline my heart to your testimonies," which, as we know from the New Testament, would only be possible with the Spirit's regenerating work.

In other words, no one in the Old Testament would have followed God at all had it not been for the regenerating work of the Spirit. In fact, Jesus seems to indicate this when, after Nicodemus expressed confusion over the notion of being "born again," Jesus retorted, "Are you the teacher of Israel, and yet you do not understand these things?" (Jn 3:10). Apparently Nicodemus should have been able to discern the doctrine of new birth from the Old Testament. Salvation in the Old Testament was by grace through faith just as in the New Testament, and these were as much a result of Spirit regeneration then as they are now.

Some theologians also refer to this act of the Spirit as "illumination," which Rolland McCune refers to as "the regeneration of the mind."[1] As I mentioned in chapter 1, this doctrine of illumination is one area where many Christians have unbiblical thinking in which they assume illumination means that the Spirit will reveal to us the meaning of Scripture. We will discuss more in the next chapter about what this act of the Spirit accomplishes for believers, but the reality is that Spirit illumination is part of the Spirit's regeneration that happens at conversion.

One of the key texts is 1 Corinthians 1:18–2:16. In this passage, Paul describes the fact that "the word of the cross is folly to those who are perishing, but to us who are being saved it is the power of God" (1 Cor 1:18). Though the concept of *illumination* or *enlightening* don't directly appear in this passage, it does clearly teach that a key difference between believers and unbelievers is the fact that unbelievers simply do not recognize the truthfulness, beauty, and authority of God's Word (specifically the gospel), while a believer is one who has come to recognize Scripture as such, not because of any human persuasion, but simply through "the Spirit and of power" (2:4).

---

[1] Rolland McCune, *A Systematic Theology of Biblical Christianity: Volume 1: Prolegomena and the Doctrines of Scripture, God and Angels* (Detroit Baptist Theological Seminary, 2009), 55.

We saw in chapter 4 that 1 Corinthians 2:10–13 speak of the *inspiration* of Scripture by means of apostles and prophets. However, verses 14–16 do touch on what we may describe as Spirit *illumination*.

> The natural person does not accept the things of the Spirit of God, for they are folly to him, and he is not able to understand them because they are spiritually discerned. [15] The spiritual person judges all things, but is himself to be judged by no one. [16] "For who has understood the mind of the Lord so as to instruct him?" But we have the mind of Christ.

The key phrase is "does not accept the things of the Spirit of God." When the natural man reads Scripture, he does not accept it as God's authoritative revelation. Rather, he sees it as foolishness. He does not understand its spiritual significance.

On the other hand, the spiritual person recognizes the Word of God for what it is and therefore submits himself to it. These verses do not speak of *intellectual* understanding but *spiritual* understanding. If we want to use the term *illumination* to describe what's going on in these verses, it refers to the Spirit's regenerating work to cause his elect to recognize the significance and authority of the written Word of God. Furthermore, this act of the Spirit is not something that necessarily happens in separate points of time as we read the Word; rather, it is something that comes as a result of the new birth—the Spirit gives us new life and enlightens our hearts and minds to recognize the significance of his Word.

In other words, 1 Corinthians 2 refers to two acts of the Spirit: *inspiration*, whereby the authors of Scripture wrote the very words of God, and *illumination*, whereby believers are enabled to recognize the spiritual significance of the Word of God.

Second Corinthians 4 makes a similar assertion, this time using explicit language of "enlightening." The gospel is "veiled to those who are perishing" (2 Cor 4:3), Paul argues. Believers accept and submit to the gospel only because God has enlightened their hearts:

> For God, who said, "Let light shine out of darkness," has shone in our hearts to give the light of the knowledge of the glory of God in the face of Jesus Christ. (2 Cor 4:6)

This is illumination—a work of God's Spirit upon a believer whereby he recognizes the beauty and glory of the gospel and therefore willingly submits himself to it. It should not surprise us that the same divine person who brought order out of chaos and light out of darkness at the beginning of time is the same one who enlightens dark hearts and brings order to disordered souls in conversion.

John Calvin argued, "Man's mind can become spiritually wise only in so far as God illumines it. . . . The way to the kingdom of God is open only to him whose mind has been made new by the illumination of the Holy Spirit."[2] An illumined believer finds value and worth in what he is reading, because it is the very Word of God. He delights in the Word of God (Ps 1:2); he *loves* God's Word (Ps 119:97). As Calvin seems to suggest, illumination begins at conversion, not as distinct occurrences later: "Christ, when he illumines us into faith by the power of the Spirit, at the same time so engrafts us into his body that we become partakers of every good."[3] From the moment our hearts are enlightened at conversion, we recognize the truthfulness and beauty of Scripture, and therefore we delight in it for the rest of our lives. An enlightened believer does not doubt or reject God's Word.

When an unbeliever reads Scripture, he may understand everything he is reading, but he simply does not recognize what he is reading to be the very words of God. An illumined believer, however, recognizes that what he is reading in Scripture is from God. As Rolland McCune argues, "illumination removes man's innate hostility toward God and Scripture and imparts intuitive certainty that Scripture is from God and is, therefore, truth and authoritative."[4]

---

[2] John Calvin, *Institutes of the Christian Religion* (Philadelphia: Westminster John Knox Press, 1960), II, iii, 20.

[3] Calvin, *Institutes*, III, ii, 35.

[4] McCune, *Systematic Theology: Volume 1*, 56.

In this sense, there really is no such thing as a believer who has not been illumined; the enlightening of the mind and heart that removes any doubt as to the truth of God's written Word occurs at the moment the Spirit regenerates a new believer. J. I. Packer observes that illumination opens "minds sinfully closed so that they receive evidence to which they were previously impervious.... It is the witness of the Spirit ... which authenticates the canon to us."[5]

This new birth immediately results in repentance and faith. Regeneration itself is experiential, but its actual effects that are experienced by an individual is his expression of repentance of sin and faith in Jesus Christ, both of which are gifts of God that result from the Spirit's regenerating work (Eph 2:8–9). First John 5:1 says that "everyone who believes that Jesus is the Christ has been born of God." Spirit-wrought regeneration has to come first—a dead heart would never respond in faith on its own (Eph 2:5), but once the Spirit brings new life, the individual will believe.

Spirit Baptism

There is some debate as to whether with Spirit baptism (mentioned 11 times in the NT) the Holy Spirit is the *agent*

---

[5] J. I. Packer, "Biblical Authority, Hermeneutics, and Inerrancy," in *Jerusalem and Athens: Critical Discussions on the Theology and Apologetic of Cornelius Van Til*, ed. E. R. Greehan (Phillipsburg, NJ: P&R, 1971), 143.

of baptism or the *medium* of baptism. If he is the *agent*, then baptism should be included also as an action of the Holy Spirit. While this is a grammatical possibility in some texts, such as the key text of 1 Corinthians 12:13, the four earliest references to Spirit baptism (Mt 3:11, Mk 1:8, Lk 3:16, Jn 1:33) predict that Christ is the one who does the action of baptizing in (*en*) the Spirit, parallel to John baptizing in (*en*) water, thus identifying the Spirit as the *medium* of the baptism. However, regardless of whether one takes the Spirit to be the *agent* or *medium*, the results are clearly articulated in 1 Corinthians 12: Spirit baptism unites all believers to Christ from the moment of their salvation and forevermore.

Because this is a highly controversial matter especially with the influence of the charismatic movement today, it deserves some attention. Let's examine the key text:

> For in one Spirit we were all baptized into one body—Jews or Greeks, slaves or free—and all were made to drink of one Spirit. (1 Cor 12:13)

First, who are the subjects of Spirit-baptism? Paul says *we all* were baptized. Who are the "we all"? All Christians. If you are a Christian, then you have been Spirit-baptized. Spirit baptism is not limited only to apostles or to super-Christians or to any subgroup within the body of Christ. We all were baptized in the Spirit.

Second, when does Spirit baptism occur? Well what is the tense of the verb here? We all *were baptized*. It is past tense. So Spirit baptism occurred sometime in the past for all Christians. And the fact that Paul can say that "we all were baptized" must indicate that Spirit baptism occurred at the moment of our salvation. If Spirit baptism took place some time after salvation, then Paul would not be able to say, "we all were baptized." Paul did not say "some were baptized," and he did not say "we will be baptized" or "we might be baptized." Paul said, "we all were baptized."

This also means that Spirit baptism happens one time, at the moment of our salvation, and it never happens again. This is true of all believers from the moment of their salvation for all time. And it also means that Spirit baptism is not something that we need to seek for, pray for, or actively receive somehow. All Christians were baptized in the Spirit the moment they put their faith in Christ. Spirit baptism is something like justification; it happens the moment we are saved, it's not something we feel or pursue; it's simply something that occurs as a result of our faith in Christ. It is not experiential, though it has dramatic effects for a believer's life.

And that leads us to the nature of what Spirit baptism is. Paul says here that we all were baptized *in one Spirit*. So the Spirit of God is like the water with which we were immersed—the word "baptize" literally means to dunk—we were all dunked with the Spirit at the moment of our salvation; in fact, Paul continues that analogy of the Spirit and water at the end of the verse when he says, "all were made to drink of one Spirit." The Spirit is the water with which we all were baptized.

Now the one question about Spirit baptism that this verse does not address is who is the one doing the baptizing? But we do have an answer to that elsewhere in the New Testament, and the earliest and perhaps best way we can answer that question is to look at the first chapter of John's Gospel.

> I myself did not know him, but he who sent me to baptize with water said to me, "He on whom you see the Spirit descend and remain, this is he who baptizes with the Holy Spirit." (Jn 1:33)

In verse 33, John the baptizer says, "I myself did not know him"—referring to Jesus Christ—"but he who sent me to baptize with water"—the word translated "with" there is the same preposition in 1 Corinthians 12:13 translated "in" the Spirit—"he who sent me to baptize with water said to me, 'He on whom you see the Spirit descend and remain, this is he who baptizes with"—same preposition—"the Holy Spirit." So John the Baptist is predicting Spirit baptism, and he specifically tells us who it is who would do the baptizing. Who is it? Jesus Christ baptized all of us with the Spirit at the moment of our salvation.

Now this, of course, leads us to the final piece of a complete understanding of the nature of Spirit baptism, and that is its results. What happened to us when Jesus Christ baptized us with the Spirit at the moment we trusted him for our salvation? At that moment, Jesus Christ immersed us with one Spirit *into one body*. So Jesus is the baptizer, and the Holy Spirit is the water, and the body of water, or the pool, or the lake into which we were all baptized is the body of Christ. Through Spirit baptism we are made one with that body.

So while Spirit baptism is a work of Christ rather than *action* of the Holy Spirit, it is nevertheless possible only because of the Spirit's unique presence in the New Covenant age. Through the Spirit, we who believe are united to Christ and to one another in Christ's body. Through the Spirit, we who believe enjoy a special communion with Christ and with the Father, along with everyone else who believes (2 Cor 13:14). As Paul clearly states, "For through [Christ] we both have access *in one Spirit* to the Father" (Eph 2:18). This is why Jesus had promised that in the day he would send his Spirit, "you will know that I am in my Father, and you in me, and I in you" (Jn 14:20).

Indwelling

As a result of the regenerating work of the Spirit, he also permanently indwells all believers. Jesus promised his disciples that he would send them "the Spirit of truth" and that he would "be with [them] forever" (Jn 14:16, 17). This abiding work of the Spirit is absolutely necessary for sanctification to take place. Paul makes this point in Romans 8, where he argues that "those who are in the flesh cannot please God." The only possible way we can please God is because "the Spirit of God dwells in you" (Rom 8:8, 9).

In 1 Corinthians 12:13, Paul argues that such an indwelling of the Spirit accompanies Spirit baptism. As we have noted, Spirit baptism occurs for all believers at the moment of their conversion, when they are immersed into the body of Christ. At that same moment, Paul argues, "all were made to drink of one Spirit," referring metaphorically to the Spirit's indwelling.

Also note that the indwelling ministry of the Holy Spirit, which is true for all Christians from the moment of their conversion, means that all three persons of the triune God indwell believers—we are "filled with all the fullness of God." In Ephesians 3:17, Paul refers to *Christ* dwelling in our hearts as a result of the Spirit's work, and indeed, Paul mentions Christ dwelling in us in Romans 8:9, Galatians 2:20, and Colossians 1:27. Jesus himself said that in sending the Spirit to his disciples, "I will come to you," and as a result, "you will know that I am in my Father, and you in me, and I in you" (Jn 14:18, 20). McCune explains, "Thus, for a believer to be inhabited by the Spirit is simultaneously for him to have the Father and the Son take up residence through the Spirit because of the godhead's mutual in-dwelling."[6] Communion with God is possible because of the indwelling ministry of the Holy Spirit of God.

This relational nature of the Spirit's indwelling should also help us avoid thinking of the Spirit's indwelling pres-ence as something *spatial* and *material*, as if a ghost pos-sesses someone's body. It is not *spatial*, but *relational*. The Spirit's indwelling presence is not about *location*, it is about his *work* within the believer's life. This *work* results in com-munion with the triune God, in assurance (see next point), and in sanctification (which we will explore more fully in the next chapter).

Assurance

The Bible also speaks of the Holy Spirit as sealing our salvation, giving us inner assurance that we are indeed children of God, which is a result of his indwelling pres-ence. Paul states,

And it is God who establishes us with you in Christ, and has anointed us, [22] and who has also put his seal on us

---

[6] Rolland McCune, *A Systematic Theology of Biblical Christianity: Vol-ume 2: The Doctrines of Man, Sin, Christ, and the Holy Spirit* (Detroit Bap-tist Theological Seminary, 2010), 332.

and given us his Spirit in our hearts as a guarantee. (2 Cor 1:21–22)

Later Paul describes the Spirit as a pledge (2 Cor 5:5). Likewise, he says in Ephesians 1:13, "In him you also, when you heard the word of truth, the gospel of your salvation, and believed in him, were sealed with the promised Holy Spirit."

This is an objective reality, but it also results in subjective, experiential assurance. Paul assures believers that "the Spirit himself bears witness with our spirits that we are children of God" (Rom 8:16). This is not through new revelation or "inner promptings," but rather through the Spirit giving us an inner confidence in God's Word and in the relationship that we have with him through the gospel.

Praise the Holy Spirit

Does the Holy Spirit of God actively work today? Clearly he does—salvation would not be possible without him. Each of these works that the Spirit accomplishes to perfect and complete the plan of the Father and the atoning work of Christ for his elect is a divine work, and these works will continue until the end of the age.

Most of these works are experiential—the believer experiences the effects of what the Holy Spirit does. He is convicted of his sin, only because of the Spirit's active work.

His mind and heart are given new life and enlightened to the beauty and truth of Christ and the gospel. The Spirit experientially indwells the believer and gives him assurance that he is now a child of God. None of these works will have immediately observable, external effects like speaking in tongues or prophecy (see chapter 8), but they are such transformative, life-altering divine acts that the person in whom the Holy Spirit does these things will never be the same.

And furthermore, though these divine acts of the Spirit are in one profound sense supernatural—they can only happen by the power of the Spirit, he accomplishes these works *through* natural means. The Holy Spirit convicts sinners (Jn 16:8), but he does so by means of the Word he inspired, which is profitable for such conviction (2 Tm 3:16).

The Holy Spirit regenerates dead hearts, but he does so by means of his Word. He does not "zap" new life in a person's heart independently of the Word—"faith comes from hearing, and hearing through the word of Christ" (Rom 10:17). Part of the Spirit's work of creating new life is putting his law within new believers and writing it on their hearts (Jer 31:33).

Likewise, the Spirit's indwelling presence is his Word dwelling within us. As we will explore more in the next chapter, the Spirit actively fills us with his Word, which results in all of the experiential benefits of his work (Eph 5:18, Col 3:16). I mentioned earlier the fact that the Spirit's dwelling within in us is often described as being filled with the fullness of the triune God (Eph 3:19), and so what Christ says about his abiding presence is true also of the Spirit. In John 15, Jesus equates his abiding within a believer with *his words* abiding within them. The same is true of the Spirit: for him to indwell a believer means that his Word indwells them.

And so it should not surprise us that the assurance the Spirit brings to a believer that he is a child of God also does not come apart from his Word. Ephesians 1:13 captures all of these works of the Spirit well and explicitly attributes them to the Word: "In him you also, when you *heard the word of truth*, the gospel of your salvation, and *believed* in him, were *sealed* with the promised Holy Spirit."

Without the work of the Holy Spirit, there would be no salvation. God the Spirit completes and perfects the plan of God the Father and the atonement of God the Son in the lives of God's elect. The Spirit brings order to disordered souls. And he accomplishes all that he does through his sufficient Word.

Don't ever think that because the Holy Spirit no longer empowers individuals in extraordinary ways or gives direct revelation that he is no longer active in his divine work. No—without the Holy Spirit, no one would come to Christ in saving faith.

We ought to marvel daily in the Spirit's incredible supernatural works in which he orders the souls of his elect and brings to completion Christ's saving work on their be-half. In fact, when we desperately long for other extraordi-nary works of the Spirit, that actually causes us to miss the wondrous ways he is at work in the saving of souls.

Praise the Holy Spirit for his amazing works in saving his people.

7

Sanctification

The Holy Spirit's characteristic work is not only an ordering of God's historical-redemptive plan, but it also a "moral ordering."[1] In the NT, the second most frequent action of the Holy Spirit after revelation is the sanctification of believers, appearing at least 24 times. This re-ordering began with salvation and continues with the Spirit's frequently mentioned work of sanctification (Rom 15:16, 1 Cor 6:11, 2 Thes 2:13, 1 Pt 1:2). Next to salvation itself, the Spirit's work of sanctification is his most significant ongoing work in this age.

Indwelling

The Spirit's indwelling presence begins at conversion and continues permanently through the life of a believer. We have seen that the Spirit's indwelling helps assure us that we are children of God, but it also refers to the work of the Spirit by which our inner beings are continually "strengthened with power" (Eph 3:16). Through the Spirit's

---

[1] Ferguson, *The Holy Spirit*, 24.

indwelling work, we are able to love Christ as we ought, resist sin, and grow in holiness. This is what Paul prays for at the end of Ephesians 3:

> For this reason I bow my knees before the Father, [15] from whom every family in heaven and on earth is named, [16] that according to the riches of his glory he may grant you *to be strengthened with power through his Spirit in your inner being,* [17] so that Christ may dwell in your hearts through faith—that you, being rooted and grounded in love, [18] may have strength to comprehend with all the saints what is the breadth and length and height and depth, [19] and to know the love of Christ that surpasses knowledge, *that you may be filled with all the fullness of God.* (Eph 3:14–19)

This ministry of the Spirit, as Paul indicates in Ephesians 3, results in an ordering of the life of a believer. That fact that our bodies are temples of the Spirit is both the critical means by which we can battle fleshly sin and an important motivator to actively do so. As Paul admonishes,

> Flee from sexual immorality. Every other sin a person commits is outside the body, but the sexually immoral person sins against his own body. [19] Or do you not know that *your body is a temple of the Holy Spirit within you,* whom you have from God? You are not your own. (1 Cor 6:18–19)

The Spirit's indwelling ministry also makes him a helper for the believer. Jesus described the Spirit as the "Helper" and "Comforter" (Jn 14:16, 26). Likewise, Paul tells us that when we are desperately weak and in need such that we groan in prayer, not even knowing exactly what to ask, the Spirit intercedes on our behalf (Rom 8:26–28).

Illumination

As is true of regeneration at the moment of conversion, the Spirit's continued indwelling presence involves the continued work of illumination. I mentioned in chapter 1 that one way we see an improper view of the Holy Spirit's work is in how many people understand the doctrine of illumination as one in which the Spirit communicates the meaning of Scripture to us or otherwise helps us understand the Bible's meaning.

But this is not what illumination means. As we saw in chapter 4, we ought not to expect the Spirit to speak to us outside of Scripture. While the term *illumination* does not appear in Scripture, it does describe a collection of concepts involving the Spirit's work in relation to his Word in the believer's life. As we already saw in the last chapter, regeneration involves the Spirit enlightening our minds and opening our eyes to the beauty of the gospel and the authority of the Word rather than giving us special insight or understanding of the Bible's meaning. Thus, illumination begins at conversion as a result of the Spirit's work of regeneration and his indwelling presence, and it continues for the duration of a believer's life as a necessary means of sanctification.

One text that refers to the continuing benefit for believers of what we may call illumination is Ephesians 1:16–23. Here Paul specifically uses the phrase "having the eyes of your heart *enlightened*" (v. 18). And what is the result of such illumination? Like with 1 Corinthians 2, the result of this enlightening is that believers continue to recognize the value and authority of the truth of God's revelation for the entirety of their lives.

> I do not cease to give thanks for you, remembering you in my prayers, [17] that the God of our Lord Jesus Christ, the Father of glory, may give you the Spirit of wisdom and of revelation in the knowledge of him, [18] *having the eyes of your hearts enlightened,* that you may know what is the hope to which he has called you, what are the riches of his glorious inheritance in the saints, [19] and what is the immeasurable greatness of his power toward us who believe, according to the working of his great might [20] that he worked in Christ when he raised him from the dead and seated him at his right hand in the heavenly places, [21] far above all rule and authority and power and dominion, and above every name that is named, not only in this age but also in the one to come.

[22] And he put all things under his feet and gave him as head over all things to the church, [23] which is his body, the fullness of him who fills all in all.

No new revelation is imparted; rather, illumination causes believers to accept God's Word for what it is—the sufficient, authoritative revelation of God.

In Philippians 3:15, Paul tells believers, "Let those of us who are mature think this way, and if in anything you think otherwise, God will reveal that also to you." Here, too, "reveal" refers not to new knowledge but to a kind of spiritual maturity that rightly submits to and appropriates God's written revelation. Likewise, in Colossians 1:9, Paul prays that believers "may be filled with the knowledge of his will in all spiritual wisdom and understanding." Again, this refers not to new revelation or even intellectual comprehension but rather to *spiritual* recognition of the significance of God's Word in the believer's life and the ability to rightly appropriate God's Word.

These texts do not describe the Holy Spirit giving believers new revelation or even new *meaning* of a biblical text. As Henry argues,

The Spirit illumines the truth, not by unveiling some hidden inner mystical content behind the revelation . . . but by focusing on the truth of revelation as it is. The Spirit illumines and interprets by repeating the grammatical sense of Scripture; in doing so he in no way alters or expands the truth of revelation.[2]

The bottom line is that Scripture is sufficient for our sanctification. The Spirit revealed the things of God to specific men who penned the Words of Scripture (1 Cor 1:10). The meaning of Scripture is in the text, and it is self-authenticating, sufficient, and authoritative. Our responsibility is simply to apply the sufficient Word to our lives.

But neither does illumination mean that we are given new understanding of the text. In other words, illumination does not eliminate the need for diligent study in order to understand Scripture—it does not give us *understanding* in an intellectual sense. We must still work to grasp the meaning of Scripture. As Paul tells Timothy, we must work diligently so that we might "rightly [handle] the Word of truth" (2 Tm 2:15).

Rather, illumination means that our enlightened minds continue to recognize Scripture as God's revelation throughout our lives. A Spirit-illumined Christian does not doubt that what God has written is the truth, though he may have to work to intellectually understand the *meaning* of what he is reading.

Spirit illumination also causes us to recognize that what we are reading in God's Word is authoritative for us. Since

---

[2] Henry, *God, Revelation and Authority*, 283.

our enlightened hearts recognize the Bible as God's revelation that is true and beautiful, we know that it has authority over us. These are not simply abstract words from God, they are words we ought to *obey*.

Illumination does not reveal to us the *meaning* of a biblical text, but it does cause us to recognize the *significance* of Scripture for our lives. Calvin notes that "by the inward illumination of the Spirit he causes the preached Word to dwell in [believers'] hearts."[3] Because an illumined believer recognizes the truthfulness and beauty of the Word, he also recognizes how important it is that he intentionally apply the Word to his life.

However, the specific ways in which we ought to apply God's Word to our lives are not going to be somehow "revealed" to us, through direct revelation, a "still small voice," or some improper understanding of illumination. We have already been illumined, and that illumination is ongoing; we must now work hard to discern ways in which our lives need to change as a result of God's sufficient Word.

As Paul prayed in Colossians 1:9, we ought to pray for "spiritual wisdom and understanding," that is, the God-given ability to rightly apply God's Word to our lives. And he will give us that wisdom. But spiritual wisdom means that *we* will be able to rightly apply the Word, it does not mean that the Spirit is going to apply it for us. The Spirit

---

[3] Calvin, *Institutes*, III, xxiv, 8.

gives us *wisdom*, he does not give us new *revelation*. As 1 Corinthians 2:14 says, by the Spirit believers are enabled to "accept the things of the Spirit of God."

Finally, an illumined believer will willingly submit to the authoritative revelation of God. This is the natural outcome of all that has come before. Believers recognize the Bible to be God's truthful, beautiful, authoritative, significant revelation, and since our hearts have been enlightened, we want to obey it.

This is not to say that we will perfectly obey or that we will not struggle with sin. But the same Spirit who enlightened our hearts at conversion also convicts us of sin, and at the end of the day, all true believers will progressively become more and more sanctified as they submit themselves to the authority of Scripture.

In sum, we could define *illumination* as "that special activity of the Holy Spirit by which man can recognize that what the Scripture teaches is true, and can accept and appropriate its teaching"[4]

Praise be to God for his Spirit's supernatural work of illumination in our hearts. Without it, we would not be able to accept the things of the Spirit of God, we would not recognize them as the truthful, authoritative revelation of God that they are, and we would not willingly submit ourselves to them.

---

[4] Henry, *God, Revelation and Authority*, 282.

But because at the moment of our conversion, our hearts were enlightened to the truths of God, we accept his inscripturated Word as God's revelation, and we work diligently to apply the truths therein, for it is God who works in us, both to will and to work for his good pleasure (Phil 2:13).

Be Filled by the Spirit

The illuminating work of the Spirit as he indwells us stresses the means by which he sanctifies us—through his Word. As we have seen, the Spirit opens our minds and hearts to accept and submit to the authority of the Word that he inspired. And thus it is through such submission to the Word that the Spirit sanctifies us. This is critically important to recognize: the Holy Spirit will not sanctify us apart from his Word.

In fact, this is exactly what is indicated when Paul commands us to "be filled with the Spirit" (Eph 5:18). Like Spirit baptism and illumination, Spirit-filling is another work of the Spirit that has been significantly confused by errant teaching, but careful attention to the biblical text will give us clarity as to the exact nature of this work of the Spirit.

In chapter 5, we saw that language of *filling* is often used to describe the special empowerment that the Spirit gave to key leaders of God's people during important periods in redemptive history. We saw that in the New Testament, these all appear in Luke and Acts, where Luke uses the term *pimplēmi*, in which the grammar clearly indicates that he is the content of the filling. These leaders were *filled with the Spirit* in a unique way that empowered them to lead God's people. In contrast, Luke uses the adjective *plērēs* five times in which the grammar indicates that the Spirit is the content of the filling and that this is a figurative expression.[5] In other words, these cases describe individuals who are characterized as being "spiritual."[6] Similarly, in one case Luke uses the verb *plēroō* in Acts 13:52 to describe the disciples as characterized by spiritual joy.[7] This is similar to when we might describe someone as being a "spiritual" person or a "godly" person. What we mean is that the person's life is characterized by qualities that identify him with qualities of God himself.

So to summarize, Luke uses two different word groups to distinguish two kinds of filling:

- *pimplēmi* refers to unique filling for special ministry
- *plērēs/plēroō* refers to ordinary filling, meaning characterized as "spiritual"

---

[5] Combs, "Spirit-Filling in Ephesians 5:18," 34.

[6] These instances are Luke 4:1; Acts 6:3, 6:5, 7:55, 11:24.

[7] Fairman, Richard G., "An Exegesis of 'Filling' Texts Which Refer to the Doctrine of Filling" (ThD dissertation, Grace Theological Seminary, 1986), 259.

Paul's command in Ephesians 5:18–19 is related to the second use but grammatically different:

> And do not get drunk with wine, for that is debauchery, but *be filled with the Spirit,* [19] addressing one another in psalms and hymns and spiritual songs, singing and making melody to the Lord with your heart.

In both cases above, the Spirit is the *content* of the filling, either in a unique sense or in an ordinary metaphorical sense. Paul uses the same verb that Luke used in Acts 13:52, *plēroō*, but with a different grammatical construction. Instead of "Spirit" being the content (genitive) of the filling, in Ephesians 5:18 "Spirit" is the object (dative) of the preposition *en* (translated in the ESV as "with"). Although this construction can indicate that the Spirit is the content of filling, Greek grammarian Daniel Wallace makes a strong case that Spirit refers to the *means* instead of *content.*[8] Andy Naselli provides helpful illustrations of the difference between content and means:

---

[8] Daniel B. Wallace, *Greek Grammar Beyond the Basics: An Exegetical Syntax of the New Testament with Scripture, Subject, and Greek Word Indexes* (Grand Rapids: Zondervan Academic, 1997), 374–75.

Illustrations of the difference between content and means[9]

Content	Means
Fill a pool with water	Fill a pool with a hose
Fill a tire with air	Fill a tire with an air-compressor
Fill one's stomach with food and liquid	Fill one's stomach with eating and drinking utensils
Fill a tooth's cavity with amalgam or composite	Fill a tooth's cavity with dental tools
Be filled with the Spirit.	Be filled by the Spirit.

In other words, in Ephesians 5:18, "Spirit" is the *means* of filling rather than the *content* of filling, and thus it would be better to translate the command as "be filled *by* the Spirit" (the Greek preposition *en* can be translated either way).[10]

So if the Spirit is the *means* of filling in Ephesians 5:18, what is the *content* of the filling? The best way to determine the answer is by looking at the parallel verse in Colossians 3:16:

Let the word of Christ dwell in you richly, teaching and admonishing one another in all wisdom, singing psalms

---

[9] Andrew David Naselli, *No Quick Fix: Where Higher Life Theology Came From, What It Is, and Why It's Harmful* (Bellingham, WA: Lexham Press, 2017), 64.

[10] It could be that Spirit is both means *and* content, just like wine is both the means and content of getting drunk. Even if Spirit is content, the rest of what I will argue below concerning Spirit-filling still applies.

and hymns and spiritual songs, with thankfulness in your hearts to God.

The command here is nearly identical to Ephesians 5:18, but instead of the command being to let the Spirit fill us, the command in Colossians 3:16 is to let the Word of Christ dwell in us richly. The implication is that these are related concepts, and thus the *content* of the filling is *the Word of Christ.*

The command of Ephesians 5:18, then, ought to be clear: *Paul commands us to let the Holy Spirit fill us with his Word.* The point is clear and is something we have noted multiple times in our study of the Holy Spirit's work: the Spirit always works through his Word. To be filled by the Spirit is to be filled with the Spirit's Word.

And, of course, this is why Spirit-filling is so crucial to our sanctification, since it is the Word that the Spirit breathed out "for teaching, for reproof, for correction, and for training in righteousness, that the man of God may be complete, equipped for every good work" (2 Tm 3:16-17). The "filling" picture embodied by the *plērēs/plēroō* word group expresses the nature of how sanctification happens. In all of those cases, the ordinary filling with/by the Spirit signifies submission to his control by his Word. Sanctification does not take place apart from the Spirit's work, but it is not passive—we must read the Word and submit ourselves to it; that is what it means to be filled by the Spirit.

Fruit of the Spirit

As we saw above, to be "filled with the Spirit" means to be characterized as spiritually mature and godly as we are more and more controlled by the Spirit as he fills us with his Word. Therefore, of particular importance for this discussion is a careful focus on what Paul calls "the fruit of the Spirit" in Galatians 5:22–23, the results of such an ordering in the life of the Christian: "love, joy, peace, patience, kindness, goodness, faithfulness, gentleness, self-control." Indeed, the overwhelming emphasis in the NT concerning what will characteristically define the life of a mature, Spirit-filled Christian is on sobriety, discipline, dignity, and self-control—Paul commands believers to "think with sober judgment" (Rom 12:3), "be sober" (1 Thes 5:6, 8), and "be self-controlled" (Tit 2:12), as does Peter (1 Pt 1:13, 4:7, 5:8; 2 Pt 1:6). In particular, he urges older men to "be sober-minded, dignified, self-controlled, sound in faith, in love, and in steadfastness," older woman to "be reverent in behavior," and younger women and men to "be self-controlled" (Tit 2:2–6).

These qualities are what characterize believers as "spiritual" because they have let the Word of Christ richly dwell in them, submitting to the Spirit's sanctifying control through his Word as he brings order and stability to the believer's life. We wouldn't really characterize this sanctifying work of the Spirit as "extraordinary experience," though it certainly is a divine work. Furthermore, contrary to what might be common expectations among evangelical Christians today, Scripture never describes the fruit of the Spirit's work in a believer's life with language like intensity, passion, enthusiasm, exhilaration, or euphoria. These are *disordered* passions.

Rather, sanctification is the result of the progressive work of the Spirit to sanctify a believer, to bring a believer's whole person into harmony with the will of God, through the ordinary disciplines of his Word. John Murray summarizes the Holy Spirit's work in sanctification: "It is the efficacious and transforming enlightenment of the Holy Spirit by which the people of God attain 'unto a perfect man, unto the measure of the stature of the fulness of Christ' (Ephesians 4:13)."[11]

Walk by the Spirit

Galatians 5:16 tells us clearly how we should respond to this understanding of how the Holy Spirit works in our sanctification: "But I say, walk by the Spirit, and you will not gratify the desires of the flesh."

Unlike salvation, which is *monergistic*, that is, the Holy Spirit does all the work in regenerating dead souls,

---

[11] John Murray, *Principles of Conduct: Aspects of Biblical Ethics* (Wm. B. Eerdmans, 1957), 225.

sanctification is *synergistic*, meaning that although sanctification would never happen apart from the Holy Spirit's active work, we have part to play as well: We must walk by the Spirit.

What does it mean to walk by the Spirit? Based on what we have seen, the answer should be evident. To walk by the Spirit is to let him fill us with his Word, and so we must read his Word. To walk by the Spirit is to pursue those qualities that characterize the Spirit, and so we must meditate upon Scripture and actively work to pursue those things. To walk by the Spirit is to allow the Spirit to lead us through his Word, and so we must meditate upon and memorize Scripture so that when we come to decisions in our lives, we will choose that which aligns with God's moral will as he has articulated in Scripture.

Let us actively walk by the Spirit, so that we will not gratify the desires of the flesh.

8

Gifting

The filling ministry of the Holy Spirit, as we saw in the last chapter, results in sanctifying believers to be "spiritual"—to be characterized by inner life and external behavior that conforms to the will of God.

However, another result attributed often to Spirit-filling in the New Testament is gifting. We have already seen that this is true with special empowerment for leadership of God's people (chapter 5). This unique gifting given temporarily to key figures like prophets and apostles often resulted in revelation, special miracles, notable power, and even less extraordinary gifting like boldness and courage. Often this empowerment, as we saw in the last chapter, was described as being "filled [pimplēmi] with the Spirit," where the Spirit is the content of the filling.

As we saw in chapter 4, it was by means of this extraordinary Spirit-filling that key individuals prophesied. And in the same way, by means of this unique Spirit-filling the disciples spoke in tongues (Acts 2:4), the disciples were given extraordinary boldness to speak the Word of God (Acts 4:31), and Paul was equipped for his apostolic work

(Acts 9:17). This kind of filling and gifting, as we have seen, is unique and ought not be something we should expect today.

Gifting for Service

But this is also true of the more ordinary Spirit-filling (*plērēs/plēroō*), where this language is used to describe the Spirit's work in every believer's life to sanctify him through his Word and equip him for service. For example, by means of this ordinary Spirit-filling, Jesus was given strength to resist temptation (Lk 4:1-2), the first deacons were equipped to serve (Acts 6:3), and Stephen was given courage in the face of death (Acts 7:55).

Furthermore, the New Testament uses several terms to describe gifts that are given by the Spirit of God to believers:

- *pneumatikon* – "spiritual gifts" (1 Cor 12:1)
- *charisma* – "grace gifts" (1 Cor 12:4; 1 Pt 4:10)
- *diakonia* – "service" (1 Cor 12:5; 1 Pt 4:10)
- *energema* – "activity" (1 Cor 12:6)
- *doma* – "gift" (Eph 4:8)
- *merismos* – "distributed gifts" (Heb 2:4)
- *phanerosis* – "manifestation" (1 Cor 12:7)

Gifting

As can be seen in the representative Scripture references listed above, many of these terms are clearly used to describe the same thing. First Corinthians 12 in particular makes this clear, where the same concept is called "spiritual gifts" (12:1), "grace gifts" (12:4), "service" (12:5), "activities" (12:6), and "manifestation" (12:7). Similarly, 1 Peter 4:10 uses both "grace gifts" and "service" to describe the same thing.

First Corinthians 12 explains that these gifts are given "through the Spirit" (v. 8) or "by the one Spirit" (v. 9), and that they are "the manifestation of the Spirit" (v. 7). Since these passages explicitly ascribe the giving of these gifts to the Holy Spirit, other passages that discuss such gifts may also safely be attributed to a work of the Holy Spirit.

Clearly 1 Corinthians 12 is a key passage that helps us to understand the nature of these gifts. Several important points can be drawn out concerning gifts of the Spirit. First, Paul emphasizes their variety (vv 4, 5, 6). The Greek word translated "varieties" in each of those cases is the word from which we get our English word, "diversity." And the word translated "apportions" in verse 11 is the verb form of the same word translated "varieties" earlier.

Second, Paul emphasizes that the Spirit gives such gifts to *every* believer: "to each" (v 7); "to one," "to another" (v 8); "to another" (v 9), "to another," "to another" (v 10); "to each one individually" (v 11). This is also clear through the rest of the chapter as he emphasizes the important function of every member of the body, each of whom has been gifted.

Third, both the use of the term *diakonia* ("service") as a term for such gifting and the whole point of Paul's discourse in this passage make clear the purpose of Spirit gifting: service within the body of Christ. He says directly in verse 7, "To each is given the manifestation of the Spirit for the common good."

Thus, we could define these gifts as Spirit-given abilities "given for service within the ministry and outreach of the local church,"[1] including miraculous gifts (e.g. prophecy, miracles, healing, and tongues) and non-miraculous gifts, which Stitzinger describes as abilities that "operate within the natural realm of order even though God's hand of providence is involved"[2] (e.g. evangelism, teaching, mercy, administration, etc.).

---

[1] McCune, *A Systematic Theology*: Volume 2, 349. Wayne Grudem, a continuationist, defines them similarly: "A spiritual gift is any ability that is empowered by the Holy Spirit and used in any ministry of the church" (Grudem, Systematic Theology, 101).

[2] Stitzinger, "Spiritual Gifts: Definitions and Kinds," 161.

Transitional Gifts

Of course, there is wide debate today concerning whether and which of these gifts continue today.[3] The chapters on revelation and empowerment above discussed the core reason I believe gifts of the Spirit have ceased: they were inherently transitional in nature. The Spirit gave revelation and empowered key individuals during important transitional periods in the progressive unfolding of God's redemptive plan. The whole purpose of the Spirit bringing order to the plan and people of God that I have been highlighting in this book reveals the inherent transitional nature of these unique works that ushered in new stages in God's redemptive plan.

The same is true with gifts like tongues and healing. With tongues, which as I demonstrated in chapter 1 is the ability to speak in known languages, the purpose was inherently transitional in nature. We have to remember that up to the time of the New Testament, God's focus had been exclusively upon the people of Israel. At the Tower of Babel God confused the languages, and from that point on the focus of his love and work was upon the descendants of Abraham, Isaac, and Jacob. Salvation was from the Jews (Jn 4:22).

---

[3] For an outstanding defense of the cessationist position, see Tom Pennington, *A Biblical Case for Cessationism: Why the Miraculous Gifts of the Spirit Have Ended* (G3 Press, 2023).

But as of Acts 2, membership in the church of Jesus Christ is not limited to one nationality. This was a concept completely foreign to a Jew, and the gift of tongues is therefore a poignant sign to the Jews that they are no longer the exclusive focus of God's attention and love—now there is no difference between Jews and Gentiles—the same Lord is Lord of all and richly blesses all who call on him. It was a sign to them that God was shifting his focus away from them for a time and toward the Gentile nations.

In fact, Paul specifically makes this point in 1 Corinthians 14, when he quotes Isaiah 28:11-12 in verse 21: "In the Law it is written, 'By people of strange tongues and by the lips of foreigners will I speak to this people, and even then they will not listen to me, says the Lord.'" The appearance of these "strange tongues" during these early years of the church was a pronouncement of curse upon the nation of Israel, and it signified to everyone that salvation was no longer held within one ethnic group.

And it is for this reason that twice more God sends the gift of tongues in the book of Acts. The second appearance of tongues comes in chapter 10 where the gospel first comes to Gentile people. Peter proclaims the gospel to Cornelius and his household in verse 34, saying, "Truly I understand that God shows no partiality, but in every nation anyone who fears him and does what is right is acceptable him." But remember, even Peter had at first been hesitant to take the gospel to the Gentiles, so God made clear that these Gentile converts were indeed part of the church, and he did so through giving them the same sign he had given in Acts 2. In verse 46 Luke records that these Gentile converts began to speak in tongues, evidencing that they, too, had been Spirit-baptized.

The third appearance of tongues in Acts 19 is similar. While Cornelius and his household were Gentile converts within Israel, in chapter 19 Paul encounters some Gentile disciples in Ephesus who had been baptized into John's baptism but apparently had not yet heard about Christ. Upon believing in Christ, they began to speak in tongues and prophesying, evidencing that Gentile converts outside Israel were, too, now part of the body of Christ.

The gift of tongues, as is evident in the three appearances in Acts along with what Paul says in 1 Corinthians 14, had a very specific purpose: it served as a sign that membership in the church was without national distinction. Furthermore, there is no biblical support for the argument that tongues in 1 Corinthians 14 were any different than those in Acts 2, and it should not surprise us that the only mention of tongues or prophecy in the New Testament epistles is in 1 Corinthians, an early Pauline letter. By the time he wrote to most other churches, those gifts had served their purpose and passed away.

The gift of healing was also transitional. Acts 2:43 specifically said that the signs and wonders were being done by apostles. In fact, 2 Corinthians 12:12 says that miracles were marks of someone who was an apostle. There are roughly thirty-three miracles in the book of Acts. Twenty-six of them are performed by apostles, and the rest are done by angels except for a few miracles done by Stephen, Philip, and Barnabas, each prominent founders of the church.

All of this information leads us to safely conclude that signs and wonders were exclusively by apostles or close associates of apostles. It is also noteworthy that every occurrence of miracles in the book of Acts is done for the benefit of unbelievers. In every case of healing in this book, it is unbelievers who are healed. But it is also evident that miracles were not performed primarily or exclusively for the benefit of the one healed. In other words, healings were not performed just so that people could be rid of their illnesses. They had a deeper purpose beyond just that. This is evident by the fact that the apostles themselves had no control over whom they would heal.

The first detailed record of a healing in the book of Acts helps us to recognize the purpose of miracles. After Peter and James heal a lame man, Peter admonishes the people,

> Repent therefore, and turn back, that your sins may be blotted out, [20] that times of refreshing may come from the presence of the Lord, and that he may send the Christ appointed for you, Jesus, [21] whom heaven must receive until the time for restoring all the things about

which God spoke by the mouth of his holy prophets long ago. (Acts 3:19–21)

That phrase "times of refreshing" is a prophetic phrase referring to the future kingdom of Christ, which, as Peter indicates, will come when Jesus comes again. Jews listening to Peter would have recognized the kinds of blessings prophesied to accompany Christ's kingdom. For example, Isaiah 35 promises that such "times of refreshing" would include blessings like plenteous, refreshing water even in wildernesses and deserts; blessings like people who at one time could not speak being able to shout for joy, or people who at one time could not walk being able to leap like a deer.

The Jews listening to Peter would have been familiar with the Greek translation of Isaiah 35, where the word "leap" in Isaiah 35:6 is the same rare Greek word Luke uses in Acts 3:8 to describe the lame man now "walking and *leaping* and praising God." Luke uses that same term again in Acts 14:10 when another lame man is healed.

The point is this: every Bible-knowledgeable Jew reading this account would recognize Luke's clear connection between this healing of a lame man and the prophecy of the coming kingdom in Isaiah 35. He used a very specific rare word that makes the connection unmistakable. And every Jew who witnessed this miraculous event would have likewise had their minds immediately drawn to the blessings promised to them in the promised kingdom, which Peter explains will come when Jesus comes again.

So healing miracles like the one in Acts 3 gave a little taste of what kingdom blessings will be like—no lameness, no sickness, only blessing. This is what is in store for those who submit to Jesus the king. Peter was calling the people to repent so that they would one day experience the times of refreshing in the coming kingdom, and the healing was exactly the kind of blessings that they knew would come with the promised kingdom.

In this way, the miracle authenticated the message of Jesus as king. There would have been no doubt in these Jews' minds—if this lame man was healed in the name of Jesus, then Jesus must be the promised king. Their only response was to reject him or submit to him.

This is the primary purpose of miracles—to authenticate the message that Jesus is king by giving a foretaste of kingdom blessings. This has been true of every period of redemptive history: miracles authenticated God's revelation at every key stage in kingdom history throughout the Old Testament. The same is true in this key transitional period in the book of Acts. As we have seen, this is exactly where the Spirit's works fit—in bringing order to God's plan of establishing his kingdom on earth with Christ as king.

At this time in the book of Acts, there was no completed Bible; there was no unified message of the Holy Spirit, and so he had to authenticate his true message through miracles in order to distinguish which messages were truly his. But now the Scriptures are finished. We have a completed Canon of Scripture. Because of this, the Holy Spirit no longer needs to authenticate his message through some kind of external means like miracles. The Holy Spirit now authenticates his completed Word directly. As 1 John 5:6 says, the Spirit himself testifies as to the truthfulness of the message of Jesus Christ. If anyone says something contrary to the Scriptures, we know it is untrue because we have a completed Bible. They did not have this privilege yet, and so the Holy Spirit had to do something external to authenticate his message.

Here is the key: Before the complete Canon of Scripture, the Holy Spirit authenticated his message through signs and wonders. Now that the Bible is completed, the Bible itself is self-authenticating, meaning that it needs nothing outside itself to authenticate its message. Since the Holy Spirit inspired the message itself, he can attest to its truthfulness through illuminating the heart of the listener, that is, removing any doubt or question as to whether or not it is true. And because the completed Bible is self-authenticating through the illumination of its Author, signs and wonders are no longer needed.

Now most cessationists claim that only so-called "miraculous" gifts have ceased, but other gifts of the Spirit continue, such as teaching, hospitality, evangelism, etc. I believe that is a perfectly acceptable position considering the purpose of the gifts. However, I will make a brief case here for why I believe *all* gifts supernaturally given by the Spirit have ceased in this age, though he continues to gift his people providentially through natural means.

This is admittedly a minority position, even among cessationists. Most who hold to a cessationist view limit the cessation of gifts only to what they describe as "miraculous sign gifts"—prophecy, healing, tongues, etc. The argument, with which I wholeheartedly agree, is that these gifts were provisional in nature, given temporarily to unique individuals like prophets and apostles at key transitional periods in the progress of God's redemptive plan. Their purpose, as I have stressed repeatedly in this book, was to bring God's people and purposes into order during times when new revelation was necessary and "epochally significant" [4] events were happening in history.

In the New Testament, Larry Pettegrew stresses that "the Spirit gave gifts to the first Christians if for no other reason than to make the transition from the old covenant program to the new covenant program as smooth as possible."[5] This is why, for example, Paul describes "signs and wonders and mighty works" as "signs of a true apostle" (2 Cor 12:12). Pettegrew's full explanation is worth quoting:

---

[4] Ferguson, *The Holy Spirit*, 224.

[5] Larry D. Pettegrew, *The New Covenant Ministry of the Holy Spirit*, Second edition (Grand Rapids: Kregel, 2001), 157.

[1] The revelational gifts, therefore, were bestowed on the apostles and prophets to explain what the church was to believe and how it was to operate in the first age of the new covenant program. [2] The miraculous gifts were given to authenticate the new covenant ministry and authority of the apostles—especially in the giving of revelation. [3] Many of the other gifts were given to enable the churches to function according to the will of God when no New Testament Scriptures were available on a widespread scale.[6]

Yet notice that Pettegrew includes in his list of temporary gifts that the Spirit gave for transitional purposes "revelational gifts," "miraculous gifts," *and* "other gifts," which would include "non-miraculous" gifts like teaching, evangelism, mercy, administration, etc.

I agree with Pettegrew for two primary reasons: First, *all* gifts described as such in the New Testament were miraculous. Consider Peter, for example, the bumbling disciple who often put his foot in his mouth during Jesus's ministry, who preached boldly and eloquently on the Day of Pentecost after he had been supernaturally empowered by the Holy Spirit. The gift itself is not usually characterized as "miraculous," but the means of gifting was certainly supernatural. Peter's ability to preach from that moment on

---

[6] Pettegrew, *The New Covenant Ministry of the Holy Spirit*, 186–87.

was not natural, learned, or developed; it was instantaneous and unexpected—it was supernatural.

Second, as Pettegrew emphasizes, even these gifts we would normally not characterize as supernatural were given to believers in the first century to bring the church into order during that transitional period moving from the old covenant era to the church age. This served the same function as the so-called "miraculous gifts," and so the more "ordinary" gifts would have ceased as well once all of the revelation necessary for the firm establishment of the church had been inscripturated.

Providential Gifts

However, this does not mean the Spirit does not give gifts to the church today. He does. But rather than gifting believers in instantaneous, supernatural ways like he did during transitional periods, the Spirit gifts believers providentially through natural means. We do not see cases, for example, of an individual who could hardly put two intelligent words together prior to his conversion, instantaneously able to preach with eloquence when he receives the Holy Spirit. Rather, what we see is God providentially gifting individuals with abilities like teaching, administration, or mercy naturally so that when those individuals come to faith, they can use those God-given gifts for ministry within the church. I agree with Pettegrew when he says,

"We today have providential abilities, talents, or gifts that parallel the gifts of the New Testament era."[7]

I think this is important because many times the assumption that the Spirit still gives believers gifts in a supernatural way today fuels the "spiritual gift" fads in which Christians take quizzes to determine what their gifts are and then assume that if some area of service is not on their list, then they shouldn't be expected to serve in that way. It also contributes to a sort of laziness in actually *cultivating* and *learning* new skills and abilities that can be used in the service of the church since the assumption is that if I don't have a particular gift from the Spirit, then there's nothing I can do about it.

No; similar to sanctification, all gifting does come from God, but we are still responsible to cultivate and grow in our God-given abilities for the edification of the body.

I also believe attempting to distinguish between "miraculous gifts" and "non-miraculous gifts" is one reason many people have a hard time accepting that only the miraculous gifts have ceased today. I understand the difficulty since such distinctions are somewhat artificial. Instead, I would suggest that *all* miraculous gifting has ceased since those gifts were temporary and transitional in nature, though God still gifts the church providentially through natural means.

---

[7] Pettegrew, *The New Covenant Ministry of the Holy Spirit*, 187.

This certainly does not limit attributing all good gifts to the Spirit of God. Indeed, "every good gift and every perfect gift is from above, coming down from the Father of lights" (James 1:17). Nevertheless, there is a difference between gifts that the Spirit gives supernaturally, and those that he gives providentially and naturally.

Here is an example to drive this point home: If I have cancer, and after months of chemotherapy and surgery I am declared free from cancer, who gets the credit? Ultimately God does. Yet God's healing did not come supernaturally; God healed me providentially and naturally by means of doctors and medicine. God gets no less credit or glory by healing me through natural means than he would through supernatural means.

Likewise, if I am enslaved to a particular sin, and after months of faithful church membership, Bible reading, and discipline I am freed from that enslavement, who gets the credit? Ultimately God does. Yet God did not instantaneously zap me with freedom from that sin; God freed me providentially and naturally by means of the spiritual disciplines of his Word. God gets no less credit or glory by freeing me through those means than he would through instantaneous delivery.

The same is true of gifts from the Spirit today. The Spirit gifts every believer with ministry abilities for the edification of the church, and he does so providentially and naturally. When an individual is converted, the sanctifying work of the Spirit motivates him to use his gifts for ministry, and the Spirit empowers him to do so faithfully. But we are still responsible to work, to learn, and to cultivate the gifts God has given us. God gets no less credit or glory, because *every* good gift comes from him.

Ordering the Body

This concept of *ordering* also describes the purpose of the Spirit's work of gifting, specifically, an ordering of the body of Christ. Paul states that "to each is given the manifestation of the Spirit for the common good" (1 Cor 12:7). And that common good, according to Paul is the unity of the body:

> For just as the body is one and has many members, and all the members of the body, though many, are one body, so it is with Christ. (1 Cor 12:12)

The whole purpose behind the Spirit gifting individual believers is so that they can function within the unified body that he is building. Whether the gifting is supernatural or providential, the result is the same. The Spirit gives gifts for the purpose of bringing order to the body of Christ.

Serve the Church

Paul explicitly connects the Spirit's giving of gifts to bringing order within the church a few chapters later, commanding, "Since you are eager for manifestations of the Spirit, strive to excel in building up the church" (1 Cor 14:12). The Holy Spirit's gifting of individual Christians with a diversity of ministry abilities serves to build up the unity of the church—many members of one body (Rom 12:5), with the goal that this body will "attain to the unity of the faith and of the knowledge of the Son of God, to mature manhood, to the measure of the stature of the fullness of Christ" (Eph 4:13). Or, to use another NT metaphor for the church, by the Spirit, believers "are being built together into a dwelling place for God," "a holy temple in the Lord" (Eph 2:21–22).

Therefore, our response to this work of the Spirit should be clear: serve the church. Don't worry about trying to figure out what your "spiritual gifts" are. Simply serve the church in any way you can. The Spirit *has* providentially gifted you to do so, so serve, and marvel at the ways the Spirit of God has uniquely gifted you to minister to others.

9

Worship

The metaphor of the Spirit building believers into a temple for God in Ephesians 2 narrows the focus of the Holy Spirit's work specifically to corporate worship. The temple metaphor is not coincidental; the gathered NT church is the dwelling place for the Spirit of God in this age in the same way that the temple was God's dwelling place in the OT economy.

As we saw in chapter 7, Paul describes the body of individual believers as "a temple of the Holy Spirit within you" (1 Cor 6:19), which refers to his indwelling presence of individual believers. But Paul also uses the temple metaphor in several texts with plural pronouns, describing the gathered church collectively:

Do you not know that you [plural] are God's temple and that God's Spirit dwells in you [plural]? (1 Cor 3:16)

What agreement has the temple of God with idols? For we are the temple of the living God; as God said, "I will make my dwelling among them and walk among them, and I will be their God, and they shall be my people. (2 Cor 6:16)

So then you are no longer strangers and aliens, but you are fellow citizens with the saints and members of the household of God, [20] built on the foundation of the apostles and prophets, Christ Jesus himself being the cornerstone, [21] in whom the whole structure, being joined together, grows into a holy temple in the Lord. [22] In him you also are being built together into a dwelling place for God by the Spirit. (Eph 2:19-22)

As you come to him, a living stone rejected by men but in the sight of God chosen and precious, [5] you yourselves like living stones are being built up as a spiritual house, to be a holy priesthood, to offer spiritual sacrifices acceptable to God through Jesus Christ. (1 Pt 2:4-5)

The church collectively is the temple of the Holy Spirit. The Spirit dwells within the gathered church in a manner distinct from his indwelling individual believers. And, as Ephesians 2:18 makes clear, this happens through the person and work of Jesus Christ "in one Spirit."

This also may be what Christ meant in John 4 when he said that God is seeking those who will "worship the Father in spirit and truth" (v. 23). Since "God is a spirit" (v. 24) and does not have a body like man, true worship takes place in its essence in the non-corporeal realm of the Spirit, which is why it is essential that the Holy Spirit dwell within the NT temple—the church—in the same way he dwelt in the temple of the Old Testament. God promised Israel that he would dwell among them (Ex 29:45), and we are told that his Spirit did so in order to instruct them (Neh 9:20; Hg 2:5). And while in the Old Testament, worship was specifically localized to that physical, Spirit-indwelt temple, "the hour is now here" (v. 23) that worship takes place wherever two or three Spirit-indwelt believers gather together, for there he is "in the midst of them" (Mt 18:20).

God of Peace

Furthermore, characterizing the Holy Spirit's work as one of *ordering* comes even more into clarity when narrowing the focus of his work to corporate worship. The key passage for this focus is 1 Corinthians 14:26-40. Apparently, Christians in the church at Corinth had similar expectations about the Holy Spirit's work in worship being extraordinary experience as contemporary Christians do.

Yet Paul corrects their expectation by emphasizing that even if the Holy Spirit works in extraordinary ways in worship, like with tongues or prophecy, "God is not a God of confusion"—in other words, disorder—"but of peace" (v. 33). The meaning of the term translated "peace" is a state of completeness, soundness, and harmony. Paul's argument here appears to be that even within a context of expecting the Holy Spirit to work in miraculous ways in Corinth, confusion and disorder are evidences that he is *not* working. As Charles Hodge noted about this passage, "When men pretend to be influenced by the Spirit of God in doing what God forbids, whether in disturbing the peace and order of the church, by insubordination, violence or abuse, or in any other way, we may be sure they are either deluded or imposters."[1] It is a God of peace who is at work in corporate worship.

This should not surprise us. From the very first work of the Spirit in creation through each of his works in Scripture, the Spirit's purpose has been one of peace—bringing completeness, soundness, and harmony to God's world and God's people. The Spirit is the beautifier of creation and the beautifier of human souls. He brought harmony through giving revelation and through inspiring Scripture. And he brings harmony to the body when peace rules therein.

We see something of this in Colossians 3, where Paul describes the church as a body where rightly ordered love "binds everything together in perfect harmony" (v. 14). How does that happen? We have already seen how. Our loves are rightly ordered by the sanctifying work of the Spirit, and we are bound together in perfect harmony as the Spirit builds us into a holy temple. Paul continues, "And let

---

[1] Hodge, *An Exposition of the First Epistle to the Corinthians*, 304.

the peace of Christ rule in your hearts, to which indeed you were called in one body" (v. 15). That peace, too, describes a wholeness, right ordering, and harmony. Again, we have seen this happens only through the work of the God of peace.

And how does the Spirit cultivate such harmony, peace, and unity of the body of Christ, his holy temple?

> Let the Word of Christ dwell in you richly, teaching and admonishing one another in all wisdom, singing psalms and hymns and spiritual songs, with thankfulness in your hearts to God. (Col 3:16)

Remember, we let the Word of Christ dwell in us richly as we allow the Spirit to fill us with his Word (Eph 5:18). This is the purpose of corporate worship. In corporate worship, the Spirit fills us with the Word of Christ, binding us together in perfect harmony, cultivating peace and order in the body as we sing to one another in psalms and hymns and spiritual songs.

The God of peace brings harmony and order to the body in corporate worship.

Disciplined Formation

This is Paul's central argument in 1 Corinthians 14, the only full chapter in the New Testament given entirely to the subject of worship. He argues that in the context of a

corporate gathering of the church—"when you come together"—the believers in the Corinthian church should desire the gift of prophecy over the gift of tongues. He summarizes his thesis in verse 5:

> Now I want you all to speak in tongues, but even more
> to prophesy. The one who prophesies is greater than the
> one who speaks in tongues, unless someone interprets,
> so that the church may be built up.

As I've argued in this book, I believe that both the gifts
of prophecy and tongues have ceased because of their temporary nature; however, what this chapter teaches about
these gifts within church gatherings reveals the Spirit's
work of bringing harmony to the body through corporate
worship. In other words, the reasons Paul gives for why the
Corinthian believers should desire prophecy over tongues
in corporate worship helps us to better understand the essence of the Spirit's work in worship.

Paul's argument is that for corporate worship, the gift
of prophecy—divine revelation from God—is more desira-
ble than the gift of tongues—which was an individual's expression of praise to God in a known language that no one
else in the congregation understood. The nature of those
two gifts is important: prophecy is from God to men;
tongues are from men to God. Prophecy is understandable
to all; tongues are only understandable to the one speaking
(if no one else in the congregation speaks that language).

Prophecy is for corporate edification; tongues are for individual expression.

Now why does Paul argue that for corporate worship, the Corinthian believers should desire prophecy over tongues? Notice the core reason Paul is making this argument throughout the chapter:

> On the other hand, the one who prophesies speaks to people for their *upbuilding and encouragement and consolation.* (v 3)

> The one who speaks in a tongue builds up himself, but the one who prophesies *builds up the church.* (v 4)

> Now I want you all to speak in tongues, but even more to prophesy. The one who prophesies is greater than the one who speaks in tongues, unless someone interprets, *so that the church may be built up.* (v 5)

> Now, brothers, if I come to you speaking in tongues, *how will I benefit you* unless I bring you some revelation or knowledge or prophecy or teaching? (v 6)

> So with yourselves, if with your tongue you utter speech that is not intelligible, *how will anyone know what is said?* For you will be speaking into the air. (v 9)

So with yourselves, since you are eager for manifestations of the Spirit, *strive to excel in building up the church.*
(v 12)

For you may be giving thanks well enough, but *the other
person is not being built up.* (v 17)

Nevertheless, in church I would rather speak five
words with my mind *in order to instruct others*, than ten
thousand words in a tongue. (v 19)

And this point really all climaxes in verse 26:

What then, brothers? When you come together, each
one has a hymn, a lesson, a revelation, a tongue, or an
interpretation. *Let all things be done for building up.*

In other words, one of the core reasons Paul insists that the
gift of prophecy was to be desired over tongues in corporate
worship is that the Spirit's purpose for corporate worship
is *edification of the whole body*, not just individual experiences.

This argument helps us understand that one of the fundamental purposes of a corporate worship service is for the
Spirit to build up and order the body. The Spirit's primary
role in corporate worship is that of disciplined formation
through his Word. We come to worship to be built up by
God's Word, to be formed into the image of Christ by God's

Word, to have our affections sanctified anew by God's Word. We come to a corporate worship service so that our responses of worship—our lives of worship—might be shaped by God's Spirit through his Word.

And notice also that Paul tells us exactly how this kind of edification in corporate worship takes place: edification in corporate worship takes place through order, not disorder. Christians in the church at Corinth assume that true worship will be spontaneous, and too much structure stifles the Holy Spirit. True worship takes place when I am uninhibited; no constraints.

But Paul is emphatic in verse 33: "For God is not a God of confusion but of peace." And remember, Paul is dealing here with Holy Spirit-given miraculous gifts. Arguing from the greater to the lesser, if the Holy Spirit worked in corporate worship through order even when he gave miraculous gifts, certainly his work is orderly once those gifts have ceased. It is a God of peace who is at work in corporate worship. The Spirit's work in corporate worship is that of *disciplined* formation.

Structure and order within a worship service does not stifle the Holy Spirit's work; he works through structure and order. Structure and order within corporate worship does not hinder our relationship with God, it builds our relationship with God. It is through structure and order that the Holy Spirit sanctifies us, edifies us, and forms us into worshipers of God.

On this basis, Paul provided clear principles for order in the Corinthian worship services, fully consistent with the Holy Spirit's ordinary activity. "Only two or at most three" people may speak in tongues in any given service, "and each in turn" (v. 27). If there is no one to interpret the tongues, "let each of them keep silent" (v. 28). Only two or three prophets should speak, others should weigh what is said (v. 29), and they should do so one at a time (v. 30). Far from expecting the Holy Spirit to sweep through the congregation, causing worshipers to be overcome with his presence, "the spirits of prophets are subject to prophets" (v. 32). Far from quenching the Holy Spirit, order within corporate worship is exactly how the Holy Spirit works, desiring that "all may learn and all be encouraged" (v. 31). Anthony Thiselton draws the necessary conclusions for order in corporate worship from this emphasis upon edification:

> Contrary to widespread popular uses of this chapter to assume an intimate connection between being inspired by the Holy Spirit and "spontaneity," the chapter as a whole places the issue of concern for the other and communicative intelligibility at the center of the discussion, and perceives the Spirit of God as "allocating" both "allotted time" and "differentiation" . . . as that which reflects God's own mode of self-giving in freedom conditioned by covenantal concern for the other. Thus "order" is not, as most or many modern writers claim, a

symptom of authoritarianism . . . but arises because, if the Spirit is genuinely inspiring the worship, patterns of worship will be characterized by the nature of God as one gives himself to the other in modes governed by temporal purposiveness, not by anarchy or by activities which minister largely to self-esteem.[2]

Thus in corporate worship, exactly because of how the Holy Spirit ordinarily works, "all things should be done decently and in order" (v. 40).

Be Filled with ... Emotion?

With orderly, disciplined formation being the expectation for how the Holy Spirit will work in worship, what role does emotion and music play in worship, and how are they related to the Holy Spirit? This question is particularly relevant since emotion and music are central to the contemporary expectation of how the Holy Spirit works.

Very simply, understanding the ordinary way the Holy Spirit works in worship leads to the conclusion that emotion and singing come as a *result* of the work of the Holy Spirit in a believer's life, not as a *cause* of the Holy Spirit's work. This is one of the primary misunderstandings of

---

[2] Anthony C. Thiselton, *The First Epistle to the Corinthians*, New International Greek Testament Commentary (Grand Rapids: Wm. B. Eerdmans, 2000), 1075-76.

many contemporary evangelicals today, who expect music to bring the Holy Spirit's experiential presence as they are filled with emotional rapture.

Calvin Stapert helpfully corrects this thinking with reference to Ephesians 5:18–19 and Colossians 3:16:

> "Spirit-filling" does not come as the result of singing. Rather, "Spirit-filling" comes first; singing is the response. . . . Clear as these passages are in declaring that Christian singing is a response to the Word of Christ and to being filled with the Spirit, it is hard to keep from turning the cause and effect around. Music, with its stimulating power, can too easily be seen as the cause and the "Spirit-filling" as the effect.[3]

"Such a reading of the passages," Stapert argues, "gives song an undue *epicletic* function and turns it into a means of beguiling the Holy Spirit." By "epicletic," Stapert refers to the expectation that music will "invoke" or call upon the Holy Spirit to appear. Stapert argues that such a "magical *epicletic* function" characterized pagan worship music, not Christian.[4]

As we saw in chapter 1, this is exactly what contemporary Pentecostalized worship expects of music. Historians

---

[3] Calvin R. Stapert, *A New Song for an Old World: Musical Thought in the Early Church* (Grand Rapids: Wm. B. Eerdmans, 2006), 19–20.

[4] Stapert, *New Song for an Old World*, 20.

Swee Hong Lim and Lester Ruth note how the importance of particular styles of music that quickly stimulate emotion rose to a significance not seen before in Christian worship. They observe, "No longer were these musicians simply known as music ministers or song leaders; they were now worship leaders." The "worship leader" became the person responsible to "bring the congregational worshipers into a corporate awareness of God's manifest presence" through the use of specific kinds of music that created an emotional experience considered to be a manifestation of this presence. This charismatic theology of worship raised the matter of musical style to a level of significance that Lim and Ruth describe as "musical sacramentality," where music is now considered a primary means through which "God's presence could be encountered in worship."[5] As Lim and Ruth note, by the end of the 1980s, "the sacrament of musical praise had been established."[6]

With this theology of the Holy Spirit, rather than using music to contribute to the goal of disciplined formation, music is carefully designed to create a visceral experience of the feelings that then becomes evidence of God's manifest presence. This results in music that must be immediately stimulating, easily arousing the senses and sweeping

---

[5] Lim and Ruth, *Lovin' on Jesus*, 18.
[6] Lim and Ruth, *Lovin' on Jesus*, 131.

the listeners into an emotional experience which they interpret to be a work of the Holy Spirit.

In contrast, when we have a more biblical expectation that the Holy Spirit is a God of peace who works to order our souls in corporate worship, the role of music and emotion take on an entirely different function. Often psalms and hymns serve as God's words to us, either directly quoting from or paraphrasing Scripture itself. As we saw from 1 Corinthians 14, this is where biblical worship must begin: God's Word that builds us up, that sanctifies into mature worshipers. This is why our music must be profoundly biblical and richly doctrinal.

And second, psalms and hymns can also give us language for our responses to God's revelation. But it is important to remember that the purpose of what we are singing is not merely to express what is already in our hearts; the purpose of what we sing is to *form* our hearts, to shape our responses toward God. The goal of this worship is discipleship—building up the body.

Furthermore, while the New Testament does describe certain "emotions" that rise out of the heart of a Spirit-sanctified believer, such as the "fruit of the Spirit," these will be characterized, not by extraordinary euphoria, but by what Jonathan Edwards calls "the lamb-like, dove-like spirit or temper of Jesus Christ." Truly Spirit-formed "religious affections," according to Edwards, "naturally beget

and promote such a spirit of love, meekness, quietness, for-
giveness, and mercy, as appeared in Christ."[7]

Contrary to caricatures, this kind of disciplined formation in worship is deeply emotional, but the music is not
intended to *stimulate* or *arouse* emotions; rather, deep affections of the soul are cultivated by the Holy Spirit through
his Word, and music gives language to appropriate responses to the Word. As we have seen, to be filled by the
Spirit is the same as "Let the Word of Christ richly dwell
within you." So that comes first: The Spirit fills us with his
Word, *then* we sing psalms and hymns and spiritual songs
that teach our hearts to express rightly those gracious affections that have been formed in our hearts by the Spirit
of God through the Word of God.

In fact, particularly because the characteristics of the
Spirit's fruit consisting primarily of qualities like dignity
and self-control (see chapter 7), care ought to be given in
corporate worship to avoid music that would cause a wor-
shiper to lose control. Historically, Christians with a biblical understanding of the Spirit's work recognized that although physical feelings are good, they must be controlled
lest our "belly" (a Greek metaphor for bodily passions) be
our god (Phil 3:19).

---

[7] Jonathan Edwards, *A Treatise Concerning Religious Affections*, New
Ed (Banner of Truth, 1978), 272.

Rather, since the Spirit cultivates reverence, dignity, and self-control within believers, music should be chosen that will likewise nurture and cultivate these qualities and the affections of the soul like compassion, kindness, humility, meekness, and patience (Col 3:12) and love, joy, peace, patience, kindness, goodness, faithfulness, gentleness, and self-control (Gal 5:23). The fact is that qualities like intensity, passion, enthusiasm, exhilaration, or euphoria are never described in Scripture as qualities to pursue or stimulate, they are never used to define the nature of spiritual maturity or the essence of worship, and they are never listed as what the Spirit produces in a believer's life.

The God of peace cultivates peace in the hearts of worshipers, not unbridled passion.

Worship and the Word

Throughout this book we have also seen that the Spirit does his work of ordering the people and plan of God primarily through the Word that he inspired, and this is no different for corporate worship. Paul stresses this in 1 Corinthians 14:36–38:

Or was it from you that the word of God came? Or are you the only ones it has reached? [37] If anyone thinks that he is a prophet, or spiritual, he should acknowledge that the things I am writing to you are a command of the

Lord. [38] If anyone does not recognize this, he is not recognized.

Paul was inscripturating direct revelation from the Lord here; carried along by the Holy Spirit, Paul was contributing to that "prophetic Word more fully confirmed," the written Word of God, which always carries the final authority. Paul highlights this as well in the fact that prophecy given in a corporate worship service had to be tested (v. 29), a standard that was exactly the same for prophecy in the Old Testament (Dt 13:1–5, 18:15–22). The Spirit works in worship, as he does in all of his works, primarily through his authoritative written Word.

If we truly want our worship to be "Spirit-led," then the way to ensure that happens is to fill our services with the Scripture that the Spirit gave us and through which he has promised to work. We ought not place priority in corporate worship upon the individual authentic expression of worshipers. Rather, the emphasis ought to be placed upon the corporate edification of the congregation as the Spirit speaks to us through his Word read, preached, prayed, and sung—everything about a Spirit-led worship service ought to mold and shape us into the kinds of people who will worship God acceptably each and every day of the week as the Spirit produces sanctified fruit within us through his Word.

Build up the Body

Because of the influence of revivalism in the nineteenth century and Pentecostalism in the early twentieth century, evangelical worship today has come to be defined primarily as private authentic experience rather than edification of the body. But understanding what the New Testament clearly teaches about the active role of the Holy Spirit in corporate worship, we ought to work to return to a more biblical understanding of worship itself.

In fact, modern evangelicalism tends to view salvation, sanctification, spiritual gifts, *and* worship as primarily private experiences. But what we need to recover is an understanding of how all of these works of the Spirit are connected to the corporate gatherings of the church. While the Spirit does absolutely work in individual lives, he does so through the body of Christ and by his Word.

In fact, the gathered worship of the Spirit-indwelt temple, the church, is the primary nexus of the Spirit's active work today. The Holy Spirit does work outside of corporate worship to be sure, but the gathered worship of God's people is where the Spirit accomplishes most of his work. In corporate worship, the Spirit convicts men of sin and assures them of pardon in Christ. In corporate worship the Spirit sanctifies his people, producing his fruit within them. In corporate worship, the Spirit's gifts are manifested as believers exercise those gifts for the building up of the body. And the Spirit accomplishes all of this in corporate worship through the Word that he produced.

So if you want to experience the Spirit's active work in your life, then look to the church. Join a faithful church, commit to faithful participation in all of its meetings, and actively seek to build up the body as God intends. In and through your active participation in the church of Jesus Christ, you will truly experience the Holy Spirit's works in your life.

Conclusion

Lots of confusion reigns today regarding how we ought to expect the Holy Spirit to work, but it does not have to be this way. Careful reading of Scripture gives us a robust picture of what should be our expectation for how the Holy Spirit works today.

The Spirit Brings Order

As we have seen throughout this book, the Holy Spirit's purpose in all he does is to bring order, to both individual Christians and to the Body as a whole. The descriptions in Scripture of the Holy Spirit's activity overwhelmingly attest to this purpose. The Spirit brought order to the material God created at the beginning of time, and he brings order to time itself in unfolding God's plan in history. He worked to bring peace and blessing to Israel as he dwelt among them in the Old Testament temple, and he does the same as he dwells within the New Testament temple. This was his purpose in special empowerment given to Israel's kings and prophets and his purpose in the foundational gifts he gave to the apostles and prophets during the formation of the church.

And that purpose remains the same today. The Spirit brings order to the disordered minds and hearts of his elect when he convicts them of their sin and gives them new life, when he unites them into the triune communion and particularly to Christ himself in his Body. He continues to order the lives of his people in empowering them to submit to his Word and be sanctified by it, conforming them to the image of Christ and producing fruit consistent with the harmony and beauty of God's character. And he builds up the unity of Christ's body through providentially gifting his people with abilities to use in service of God and one another in the church, particularly in corporate worship, where he forms his people through filling them with his Word read, preached, prayed, and sung.

The Spirit Works Through His Word

One of the most influential and long-lasting works of the Holy Spirit to bring order to his people was the inspiration of his Word; this is why the most frequently described act of the Holy Spirit in Scripture is the giving of revelation, and why, as we have seen, his work of "filling" a believer (Eph 5:19) is paralleled in Paul's writings with the Word of Christ "richly dwelling" within a Christian (Col 3:16). Thus, believers should expect that the Holy Spirit will work today primarily *through* his Word, and he will never act *contrary to* his Word.

For this reason, we must never conceive of any work of the Spirit today apart from his Word. If we expect the Spirit to do something apart from Scripture, we will inevitably subordinate Scripture itself to a subjective experience. We may say we believe Scripture to be sufficient, but ultimately we will ignore the objective Word, always seeking for subjective experiences, feelings, "inner voices," or impressions that we assume to be the Spirit's illuminating work. Likewise, we will also find ourselves frustrated when we don't experience some sort of feeling that we assume to be the Spirit's work. We will wonder why he isn't "speaking" to us.

Rather, we must recognize that he has already spoken to us through his sufficient Word—we ought not expect any further revelation. We must simply pray that he gives us wisdom to appropriate his Word and then actively apply and submit ourselves to what he has already spoken.

Further, if we don't properly understand how the Spirit works through his Word, when we come across a difficult passage of Scripture, instead of studying diligently and seeking the teachers God has gifted to his church, we will become frustrated. *Why isn't the Spirit helping me understand this text?*

Even Peter acknowledged that some passages of Scripture are "hard to understand" (2 Pt 3:16). The Spirit is not going to somehow make them less difficult, but he will give us such a love for Scripture that we want to be taught and to engage in our own diligent study so that we may understand. Through illumination, the Spirit has already removed what is the most significant impediment to spiritual understanding—a heart veiled by depravity.

The Spirit Works through Ordinary Means of Grace

The sufficiency of the Spirit-inspired Word of God leads also to the conviction that he has given the church in that Word all the revelation necessary concerning the means by which the Spirit will work:

The Spirit commands us, in the context of teaching him how to behave in the house of God, "devote yourself to the public reading of Scripture (1 Tm 4:13). He repeats similar commands in Colossians 4:16 and 1 Thessalonians 5:27.

The Spirit also commands pastors to "devote yourself . . . to exhortation, to teaching" (1 Tm 4:13) and "preach the Word; be ready in season and out of season; reprove, rebuke, and exhort, with complete patience and teaching" (2 Tm 4:2).

The Spirit commands that "supplications, prayers, intercessions, and thanksgivings be made for all people, for kings and for all who are in high positions (1 Tm 2:1). He commands the Colossians to "continue steadfastly in prayer (4:2), and to the Ephesians he admonishes, "praying at all time in the Spirit, with all prayer and supplication . . . making supplication for all the saints" (6:18).

Conclusion

In both Ephesians 5:19 and Colossians 3:16, the Spirit commands gathered believers to sing psalms, hymns, and spiritual songs, thereby "singing and making melody to the Lord with your heart" (Eph 5:19) and "teaching and admonishing one another in all wisdom" (Col 3:16).

The Spirit recorded Christ's command in his Great Commission to the disciples, "Go therefore and make disciples of all nations, *baptizing them* in the name of the Father and of the Son and of the Holy Spirit."

And finally, Paul told the Corinthian church that he passed on "the Lord's Supper" to the church, having received it from the Lord himself (1 Cor 11:20, 23).

In other words, the Holy Spirit inspired the sufficient revelation concerning the elements of gathered worship, and so we should expect that he would naturally work through those elements—reading the Word, preaching the Word, praying the Word, singing the Word, and visualizing the Word through baptism and the Lord's Supper.

This is why Christians have traditionally called these prescribed elements the "ordinary means of grace"—these are the primary means Christians should expect the Holy Spirit to ordinarily work his grace into our lives. Thus, Charles Spurgeon's catechism reads, "The outward and ordinary means whereby the Holy Spirit communicates to us the benefits of Christ's redemption, are the Word, by which souls are begotten to spiritual life; baptism, the Lord's

Supper, prayer, and meditation, by all which believers are further edified in their most holy faith (Acts 2:41-42; Jas 1:18)."[1]

And so, we should expect the Holy Spirit's ordinary work to be that of sanctifying us through the effectual means of grace that he has prescribed in his Word. The regular, disciplined use of these means of grace progressively forms us into the image of Jesus Christ; these Spirit-ordained elements, what Robert Letham calls "God's prescribed vehicles through which he communicates his mercies to us by the Holy Spirit,"[2] are the means through which Christians "work out [their] own salvation with fear and trembling, for it is God who works in [them], both to will and to work for his good pleasure" (Phil 2:12-13).

If we fail to trust the Spirit to work through the ordinary means he prescribes, we will fall into methods of sanctification and worship that actually *hinder* the Spirit's work of sanctification and building up of the body. This is evident with those who are otherwise committed to the sufficiency of Scripture, but nevertheless expect the Spirit to work in extraordinary ways. Inevitably they tend toward manipulative methods, especially worship music, that they assume

---

[1] Question 71 (Charles Spurgeon, *Spurgeon's Catechism*, 1855).

[2] Robert Letham, *Union with Christ* (Phillipsburg: P&R Publishing, 2011), 139.

is necessary for the Spirit to work, but in reality encourage immaturity and disorder among God's people.

Worship the Spirit

While the Holy Spirit of God, who with the Father and the Son should be worshiped and glorified, may certainly do whatever he pleases in the world, he is not a God of disorder, but a God of peace. The testimony of Scripture concerning the ordinary ways he works and a careful study of the New Testament's explicit treatment of his ordinary work in worship should lead Christians to expect, not extraordinary experience when the Holy Spirit works, but harmony, peace, and order.

Let us worship God the Holy Spirit, who shapes, guides, and fills us with his Word, by which he brings our lives into order and harmony with the good purposes and will of God.